A Mother to My Mother

THE AZRIELI SERIES OF HOLOCAUST SURVIVOR MEMOIRS: PUBLISHED TITLES

A Mother to My Mother

Malka Pischanitskaya

THE AZRIELI FOUNDATION · www.azrielifoundation.org
THE HOLOCAUST SURVIVOR MEMOIRS PROGRAM · Publisher, Naomi Azrieli · Director, Jody Spiegel · Managing Editor, Arielle Berger

Edited by Arielle Berger and Devora Levin · Book design by Mark Goldstein · Cover by Endpaper Studio · Cover image by Alex Linch · Endpaper maps by Martin Gilbert · Interior map by Merritt Cartographic · Photos on page 114 courtesy of Yad Vashem Photo Archive, Jerusalem, IDs 14473067 and 14480373 · See the acknowledgements for artwork credits.

LIBRARY AND ARCHIVES CANADA CATALOGUING IN PUBLICATION

A Mother to my mother/ Malka Pischanitskaya.
    Pischanitskaya, Malka, 1931– author. Azrieli Foundation, publisher.
The Azrieli series of Holocaust survivor memoirs; XVI
Includes bibliographical references and index.

Canadiana (print) 20240360508 · Canadiana (ebook) 20240360532
ISBN 9781998880133 (softcover) · ISBN 9781998880157 (PDF)
ISBN 9781998880140 (EPUB)

LCSH: Pischanitskaya, Malka, 1931– LCSH: Holocaust survivors — Ukraine — Biography. LCSH: Jews — Ukraine — Biography. LCSH: Holocaust, Jewish (1939–1945) — Ukraine — Personal narratives. LCSH: Mothers and daughters — Ukraine. LCSH: Immigrants — Canada — Biography. LCGFT: Autobiographies.

LCC DS135.U43 P57 2024   DDC 940.53/18092—dc23

PRINTED IN CANADA

Contents

Series Preface:
In their own words…

In telling these stories, the writers have liberated themselves. For so many years we did not speak about it, even when we became free people living in a free society. Now, when at last we are writing about what happened to us in this dark period of history, knowing that our stories will be read and live on, it is possible for us to feel truly free. These unique historical documents put a face on what was lost, and allow readers to grasp the enormity of what happened to six million Jews — one story at a time.

    David J. Azrieli, C.M., C.Q., M.Arch
    Holocaust survivor and founder, The Azrieli Foundation

Since the end of World War II, approximately 40,000 Jewish Holocaust survivors have immigrated to Canada. Who they are, where they came from, what they experienced and how they built new lives for themselves and their families are important parts of our Canadian heritage. The Azrieli Foundation's Holocaust Survivor Memoirs Program was established in 2005 to preserve and share the memoirs written by those who survived the twentieth-century Nazi genocide of the Jews of Europe and later made their way to Canada. The memoirs encourage readers to engage thoughtfully and critically with the complexities of the Holocaust and to create meaningful connections with the lives of survivors.

Millions of individual stories are lost to us forever. By preserving the stories written by survivors and making them widely available to a broad audience, the Azrieli Foundation's Holocaust Survivor Memoirs Program seeks to sustain the memory of all those who perished at the hands of hatred, abetted by indifference and apathy. The personal accounts of those who survived against all odds are as different as the people who wrote them, but all demonstrate the courage, strength, wit and luck that it took to prevail and survive in such terrible adversity. The memoirs are also moving tributes to people — strangers and friends — who risked their lives to help others, and who, through acts of kindness and decency in the darkest of moments, frequently helped the persecuted maintain faith in humanity and courage to endure. These accounts offer inspiration to all, as does the survivors' desire to share their experiences so that new generations can learn from them.

The Holocaust Survivor Memoirs Program collects, archives and publishes select survivor memoirs and makes the print editions available free of charge to educational institutions and Holocaust-education programs across Canada. They are also available for sale online to the general public. All revenues to the Azrieli Foundation from the sales of the Azrieli Series of Holocaust Survivor Memoirs go toward the publishing and educational work of the memoirs program.

∼

The Azrieli Foundation would like to express appreciation to the following people for their invaluable efforts in producing this book: Marisa Antonaya, Judith Earnshaw, joy Fai, and Inna and Mark Turner.

Editorial Note

The following memoir contains terms, concepts and historical references that may be unfamiliar to the reader. English translations of foreign-language words and terms have been added to the text, and parentheses have been used to include the names and locations of present-day towns and cities when place names and borders have changed. The editors of this memoir have worked to preserve the author's voice and stay true to the original narrative while maintaining historical accuracy. Explanatory footnotes have been added for clarification or to provide key information for understanding the text. General information on major organizations, significant historical events and people, geographical locations, religious and cultural terms, and foreign-language words and expressions that will help give context to the events described in the text can be found in the glossary beginning on page 119.

Introduction

"I was brought to this world not by chance, but, I believe, by destiny.…
My destiny was to be born, to endure the sufferings that were yet to
come."

This memoir is the story of one Jewish child, a girl whose destiny was
to be born and live as a Jew during a time when being a Jew was a
threat to one's very existence. Yet it is also a universal lesson on how
so many Jewish children's destinies have been defined by their ethnic-
ity over time. *A Mother to My Mother* is a personal story of surviving
the Nazi genocide in Ukraine, which at that time was a republic under the control of the Soviet Union. It is one person's experience, but
it encapsulates the power of the faith of thousands of Jewish children,
those who survived as well as those who were murdered. It speaks
for those who are not here today to share their own stories, and it
represents the experiences of so many children who have been forced
to live in lands of conflict and loss, too many of whom are still living
like this today.

Malka Pischanitskaya was a young girl from a small town called
Romaniv in today's Ukraine (previously known as Romanov, under
the Soviet regime) when World War II began. Her narrative introduc-
es the reader to what is known in Holocaust studies as the Holocaust
by bullets, a reference to the shooting massacres perpetrated by the

Nazis and their collaborators against 1.5 million Jews in Ukraine between 1941 and 1944. The term was coined by Father Patrick Desbois,[1] a Catholic priest and founder of the organization Yahad-In Unum, which is dedicated to recording the testimonies of survivors and, crucially, witnesses in order to investigate and document this history.[2]

More than eighty years after Malka's traumatic experiences of survival, she bravely and generously shares her memories with readers in words and in images, not only reflecting on the details of her survival but on the life her family lived before the genocide, the vibrancy of a Jewish community in a small town in Ukraine before the Holocaust. Her memoir will help today's generation understand the depth of the tragedy of World War II.

Before the start of World War II, the town of Romaniv was a typical Jewish shtetl — a large Jewish community that primarily spoke Yiddish — that was part of the Zhytomyr region of the Ukrainian Soviet Socialist Republic, which formed part of the larger USSR. The Soviet policy of russification and assimilation of local populations into the newly created Soviet republics often manifested itself in the renaming of settlements and streets from local languages and heroes into Russian names and identities. By forcing a new language and collective memory onto every occupied territory, the Soviet oppressors perpetuated a cycle of imperialism and colonization that was replicated throughout the Soviet Union in a veiled attempt to create a sense of unity.

---

1 Father Patrick Desbois, with a foreword by Paul A. Shapiro, *The Holocaust by Bullets: A Priest's Journey to Uncover the Truth behind the Murder of 1.5 million Jews* (New York: Palgrave Macmillan, 2008).

2 For detailed information on the Holocaust by bullets and history of the genocide in Ukraine see the Mémorial de la Shoah's online exhibit at: https://www.memorialdelashoah.org/upload/minisites/ukraine/en/en_exposition1.htm and the United States Holocaust Memorial Museum's online conference presentations *The Holocaust in Ukraine: New Sources and Perspectives* at: https://www.ushmm.org/m/pdfs/20130500-holocaust-in-ukraine.pdf (accessed April 26, 2024).

Romaniv was no exception, as under Soviet occupation its original Ukrainian name of Romaniv forcibly became Dzerzhynsk, named in the 1930s to commemorate the Soviet politician Feliks Dzierzynski, who had been a close ally of both Lenin and Stalin. A multicultural regional centre, before World War II the town supported many diverse communities, including Ukrainians, Poles, Czechs and Germans, with Jews making up a significant portion of the local population in the interwar period. According to the 1939 census, 1,720 Jews lived in the town, but by the end of the war it had become a purely mono-ethnic site of war-ravaged Ukrainians.

As Malka's story unfolds, so does the history of Ukraine, the Soviet Union, World War II and what came after. We can say we know these details as facts and figures recorded by the "winners" in history, but Malka opens a window for us to live in a world that has long been hidden by the official data.

The first chapter of the memoir, *Quiet Sorrows*, takes us back to the Soviet period, a time of widespread totalitarianism and restrictions. Malka recalls the 1930s, in particular the time of the 1932–1933 Great Famine, in a rather fragmentary way. In the 1930s, Romaniv and its surrounding regions suffered horrendously during the Great Famine. Her brief recounting of the family's experiences of the famine are understandable, for Malka was born in 1931 and would only have been a toddler when the famine started. Her memories of being a starving two-year-old may have diminished over time, yet Malka is still able to meaningfully describe her family's struggles.

The oral histories of survivors who lived in the USSR during the Great Famine reflect what can be called a double trauma in relation to hunger. First, they experienced the threat of starvation as part of the Soviet-engineered Great Famine, only to suffer the same trauma a decade later when the Nazis invaded Ukraine and began to weaponize food. In order to survive during this time, residents had to develop the strategic skills of hunting for and storing food.

This double trauma is evident in Malka's memories. When I asked her about the Great Famine, she shared some details that show the family's ingenuity, including the story, passed down through oral history within her family, that her great-aunt worked as a chef in a restaurant and learned how to smuggle spare food home to family members to keep them from starving.

Children strongly depend on their parents or close family members, and any child's world is deeply intertwined with their family's dynamic.[3] The first part of Malka's story, her childhood, shares her family's ways of expressing and showing emotion, and she warmly describes the special place she holds in her heart for her grandmother Meiti Kantor and great-aunt Gitl Kantor, who took care of her.

Malka's mother, Brindl, worked out of town, so Malka would not have known her mother well in her earlier years. Survivors often try to explain and justify their loved ones' actions and decisions, and here Malka is no different from others whose parents had to make impossible choices. Malka's mother was unable to be with her daughter every day, to raise her and be there for her, because she was forced to play a double role as mother and father, the family breadwinner. Malka's father left the family before she was born, and thus, her relationship with the person she refers to as her "so-called father" is extremely complicated, rooted in feelings of abandonment and rejection.

Malka grew up as an only child in a community of love, care and safety. Meiti and Gitl protected Malka and acted as her teachers, mothers and best friends, raising her in a culture steeped in Jewish traditions. Her family was Orthodox, and she spoke Yiddish well. Malka's descriptions of her family, friends and religious life paint an invaluable portrait of shtetl life in Ukraine before the war, giving rare

---

3 Irina Rebrova, *Oral Histories about the Daily Life Experiences of Children during World War II*, in *Children and War: Past and Present*, edited by Helga Embacher et al. (Solihull, West Midlands, England: Helion & Company, 2013), 89.

insight into Jewish community life in Romaniv and throughout the Zhytomyr region. Her family was deeply spiritual, with a strong faith in God, miracles, blessings and punishments, and tried to live their lives accordingly, with a special commitment to works of charity.

In the chapter *Changing Seasons,* Malka provides more snapshots of a life lived in tandem with the Jewish calendar. The reader has the opportunity to witness traditional holy days such as Purim, with its plates of mouth-watering poppy seed pastries known as *haman-taschen,* as well as travel with Malka through the seasons that represent Jewish life in Ukraine — Purim, Passover, Yom Kippur, Hanukkah and the Sabbath, all accompanied by the preparation of special meals. These are precious memories that can never be taken away from Malka and, perhaps, thinking back to the joy of her life before the war helps her to deal with the trauma of her life during the war.

Malka's depictions of such strong faith and traditions paint a multifaceted picture of the Jewish community's deep ties to their land and the culture that came from it. An episode from Malka's childhood that shows the power of this faith is when Malka's grandmother prayed for Malka's recovery from pneumonia, which she miraculously healed from after her grandmother followed certain Jewish rituals. As Malka grows up with Jewish customs and traditions, she remains a believer in the power of prayer and miracles. This belief would go on to serve her at her most desperate and vulnerable moments, keeping both her and her mother alive against the worst of obstacles.

By 1938, refugees from Poland began finding their way into Ukraine, sharing stories of Hitler's terror. I had always wondered why Ukrainian Jews did not leave Romaniv, and other nearby areas, when it was invaded in 1941, knowing from Polish refugees what kind of persecution might be in store for them, and I posed this question to Malka during one of our conversations. Her response was breathtaking in both its honesty and universality: "*We didn't believe that it could happen to us.*" This hope, or denial, was common among many Jewish people in Nazi-occupied territories, who simply could not foresee the atrocities to come and therefore never believed that leaving was necessary.

The Nazi invasion of the Soviet Union was devastating for so many. As Malka expresses it, "On June 22 [1941] ... people's dreams were broken." In a single day, Malka's peaceful and happy childhood was transformed into an unending nightmare. Evacuation seemed to be the only choice for many – to survive by escaping. Still, not every family could make this choice, as some refused to leave their properties and others — the disabled, the ill, the elderly — did not have the same resources or abilities that would allow them to leave. One pathway to leave was open to those who held jobs in the government civil service, as those working in positions with high levels of security were often given chances to leave due to the strategic importance of their work. Although, due to her mother's employment, Malka's family was one of the lucky ones who had a chance to leave just before the Germans came to Romaniv, they were ultimately unable to flee.

Along with her family, Malka was thrown into the terror of living in a country under Nazi control. How could she understand this new reality, this lunacy and madness of the war? What possible tools could she find to stay sane and survive? The new Nazi order defined the lives and existence of all Jews. Random police searches and arrests, and being forced to live in restrictive ghettos, were just some of the traumas that impacted both their physical and psychological states. Malka witnessed the first mass shooting of people close to her, and the sounds of gunfire and police raids intensified her fear of death.

From the beginning of the war, Malka was overwhelmed with fear. Children, due to their innocence, and lacking strength and resources to fight, were an easy target for destruction. The most vulnerable of the Nazis' targets, children were forced to grow up too fast, forced into conditions where, absent of choices, they became responsible for themselves and, sometimes, their families. The Holocaust tragically destroyed their childhoods, robbing them of safety, freedom and happiness.

Oral history testimonies of child and adult survivors often differ in how perceptions of the tragedy are remembered and thus represented. Adults understood the consequences of resisting the occupying regime and had to make life-or-death decisions while trying to keep their children safe. Children often witnessed their parents' different reactions and emotional states, which influenced their perception of their parents. Adults' reflections of the war, filtered through their individual life experiences, give a different perspective than a child's view of life at war.

On Malka and her mother's journey, they met those who gave a helping hand, risking their lives and those of their families, but, unfortunately, there were also those who betrayed them. The local population knew their neighbours well, which made it easier for the Germans to manipulate neighbours ready to inform on each other. There were also cases when collaborators changed their behaviour, turning from criminals to temporary saviours, which we see in a key turning point when Malka and her mother face a local chief of police.

Family ties often influenced decisions made within the family. In one critical moment, Malka's mother tells her to run to a friend's home, leaving her behind. This lack of choice devastated Malka, as she writes, "Leaving my mother and aunt was the hardest thing for me to do."

We will never know how Malka's mother felt, seeing her only child run away from her. Life under the constant real and psychological threat of genocide is unimaginable. We see only an inkling of how this trauma might have impacted Malka's mother: "Life did not mean anything to my mother anymore; any meaning had been lost after the first massacre. She was fighting against negative thinking only because of concern for me."

So many children who lived through the Holocaust witnessed and suffered from the public humiliation of their parents and their inability to be the protectors they should have been. As children, they perceived these incidents with shame and saw their parents as weak, not always entirely understanding the context of occupation and violence the families were caught in. In this vicious cycle, Malka witnessed her mother's mental health rapidly decline. In Malka's perception, "…children do not understand circumstances as much as adults. Pain cuts deeper into an older person's heart. This is why I knew, right then, that I would have to keep taking on the role of a mother to my mother."

Some children living under debilitating conditions, like Malka, had to take on adult roles, making vital decisions and taking responsibility for things normally the duty of adults. Searching for food or a place of refuge became daily lessons in ways to survive. Due to their age and ability to appeal to adults' heartstrings, and because they were less easy to identify as Jews, it was often easier for children to find food, as they could ask local residents, who often looked on them with kindness and shared what they could. In Malka's case, speaking Ukrainian fluently undoubtedly helped.

As Malka recalls, while her mother made the decision to escape to a village or to hide at a friend's house, Malka was the one who went in search of food each day, not knowing which door might be open to her and where she might face betrayal. When they needed to find a new shelter, Malka looked for places to hide by knocking on strangers' doors, in the hope of meeting a kind person who would take in a desperate mother and child. Her faith was constant, and she never gave up.

Malka was determined to live, and used any opportunity she could find to survive. She became responsible not only for her own life, but also for the life of her mother. Each day, in every moment, a little girl had to become an adult and make adult survival decisions. She depended not only on the kindness of neighbours and strangers, but most of all on her faith and prayers.

So many Holocaust survivors tell us that prayer and the simple belief in kindness are what kept them going through the genocide, and Malka's story is a testament to that strength as well. Despite Malka's unbearable fear, she fought to maintain her sense of self and her faith in humanity. Malka's memoirs offer us a poignant reflection on the universal value of humanity and its importance, regardless of what is happening around us. Malka and her mother tread on paths of fear, despair, betrayal, violence and hunger, but ultimately found life-saving help. Miraculously, they survived.

Malka writes of generations of women who held deep meaning in her life, who became mothers and sisters to each other through countless acts of courage and selflessness. Her narrative is multi-layered — not only the story of her own unique life, but also a much broader story of women's experiences, in which taking responsibility for vital decisions illuminates women's wisdom and courage. It is both a woman's story and a child's story, and it draws on the history of the Holocaust in a small town in Ukraine, the history of the Jewish community before the war, the history of human behaviour, of antisemitism, and, ultimately, of salvation.

When I first met Malka, I met a ninety-three-year-old woman who was deeply kind. She told me her story, one that was first painted into pictures as part of a healing workshop for survivors and is now written on these pages, giving us all a map for our own personal journeys of healing. Yes, Malka's story is the story of a little girl whose life was filled with fear and the pain of losing her family and friends. But it is also the story of a woman who found a form of salvation and redemption.

Malka remains a courageous and strong woman with a big heart and faith in the goodness of all people. Despite her suffering and pain, she has managed to live a life that preserves a deep trust and faith in what unites us instead of what divides us. Kindness and faith are the human values that helped Malka survive and she still keeps them in her heart today. It is an honour to be able to revisit and reclaim those values by bearing witness to her life and work in the pages she has written for us.

A Mother to My Mother raises important questions about the fate of children in wartime — about the conditions imposed on them, about what they had to do to survive and, most importantly, about how all these experiences impacted their lives as adults. These are questions many of us, especially those descended from survivors, are still grappling with today. This memoir takes a valuable place within Holocaust literature and memoirs, as it has the potential to reach audiences for whom the Holocaust may be nothing but a distant topic taught in textbooks. It can bring to life experiences many young people have only vaguely heard of, making Malka and her words a piece of living history. It is not only our honour, but our responsibility, to take her words into our hearts and use them to inform our actions, so that collectively we can truly say the words "never again" and know that we mean it.

Nataliia Ivchyk
PhD in History, Associate Professor in the Department of Political Science, Rivne State University of Humanities (Ukraine)
Visiting Scholar in the Department of History, University of British Columbia (Canada)
2024

Foreword

During the 31st Annual World Federation of Jewish Child Survivors of the Holocaust and Their Descendants Conference in 2019, the Vancouver Holocaust Education Centre (VHEC) was honoured to present an exhibition of artwork depicting Malka Pischanitskaya's experiences as an eyewitness to the Holocaust in Ukraine. Curated by Wendy Oberlander and titled *Romanov: A Vanished Shtetl — A Living Monument in Art and Words*, the exhibition featured nineteen vivid tableaus that animated Malka's memories of shtetl life, the brutality of the Nazis and their collaborators against the Jewish population of Romanov and the story of Malka's unlikely survival in hiding — thanks in part to the bravery of a precious few righteous individuals. The series ended with a tribute to Malka's murdered family members and a work titled *I Was the Mother to My Mother*, a theme at the heart of this memoir.

The paintings and accompanying text reflected two decades of collaborations with visual artists, who worked in partnership to transform Malka's memories into works that attempt to convey the depths of horror endured by Malka and her mother during the war. With multiple frames reaching across a single canvas, the paintings depict the terrifying experiences of a child who defied the odds again and again. The exhibition was created as an act of remembrance for those who suffered during the Holocaust and for those who did not survive. This exhibition fulfilled the central Jewish obligation: *zachor* — to remember.

Now, five years later, Malka's monumental memory project is embodying a new form and reaching new audiences. In unsparing detail, Malka's words reflect a precision and urgency, conveying her lived experiences and the complexity of family members and people she encountered during the wartime years, who reflected the worst and, in rare cases, the best of humanity. Significant themes — the richness of prewar Jewish life, the collaboration of local populations with the Nazis, the motivations of those who helped their Jewish neighbours at great personal risk and the possibility of faith in the face of a moral universe upended — are explored with candour and nuance.

As a Holocaust educator, I am acutely aware that each survivor account is unique, offering an invaluable illumination of events that defy imagination and providing a tangible, human entry-point into history. Malka's memoir feels particularly fresh because it captures a perspective of remarkable rarity — that of a child survivor of what is today known as "the Holocaust by bullets." Events in Ukraine recounted by Malka speak to the first phase of the Holocaust, in which an estimated 1.5 million Jews were shot to death at close range in ravines, open fields and forests.

That a ten-year-old child would escape and survive in hiding and on the move for more than two years amid this devastation is unlikely and perhaps, as Malka suggests, one of several miracles that defined her life. Perhaps more unlikely still is that this child would have a photographic memory and profound insights into her experiences and their meaning, as well as the courage and conviction to share these with the world.

We are all enriched by Malka's courage and conviction. For members of the local Child Holocaust Survivor Group, which meets regularly at the Vancouver Holocaust Education Centre, Malka is a deeply respected friend who never misses an opportunity to listen carefully and share words of wisdom. For the professional team of the VHEC,

Malka is our neighbour and a warmly anticipated visitor whenever she comes into the Centre. Malka's multi-year project has engaged several community members — including joy Fai, Wendy Oberlander and Adele Rich — who have dedicated countless hours to supporting documentation efforts central to Malka's visual and written testimonies.

To witness the love of Malka for her daughters, sons-in-law and grandchildren — and their love and admiration for her — is deeply moving. This tenderness between family members is beautifully conveyed within these pages, in Malka's words and in the photographs at the end of this volume.

The Vancouver Holocaust Education Centre is profoundly grateful to the Azrieli Foundation for publishing this memoir, and to Malka for her tireless commitment to memory. Thank you, dear Malka, for gifting us with your message of love and your belief in the power of faith and education to change the world.

Nina Krieger
Executive Director, Vancouver Holocaust Education Centre
April 2024

Acknowledgements

The artwork in this memoir was conceptualized by the author, Malka Pischanitskaya, and painted by various artists:

Pages xxx, 3, 8, 18, 26, 35, 39, 46, 48, 68, 72 and 78 by Veronika Mcleod.
Page 10 by Gennadiy Zhukov.
Page 13 by Elena Zhukova.
Page 22 by Katerina Goldshtein.
Pages 29 and 96 by John Zhao.
Pages 100 and 103 with Linda Dayan Frimer.

The cursive script on the paintings on pages 22, 29, 96 and 103 was written by Ava Lee Millman Fisher z"l.

The text in the chapters *Leaving Home* and *Epilogue: My Childhood Through Art* was written with the assistance of joy Fai.

Biblical quote on page 64 from Ezekiel 39: 22–29; on page 66, from Isaiah 43: 1–4; on page 75, from Isaiah 49:6.

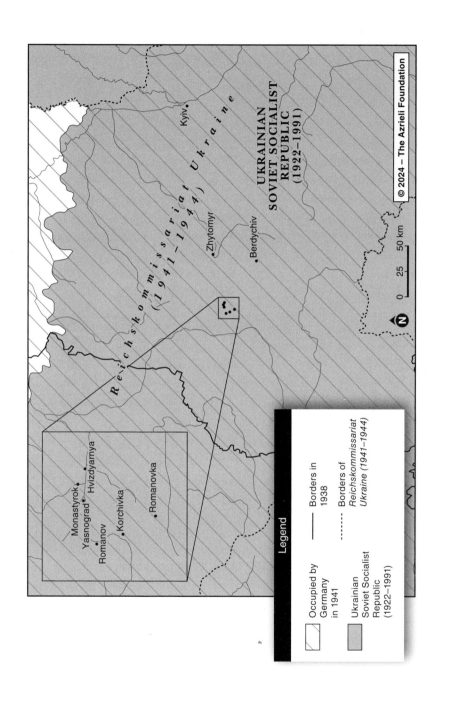

Legend

—— Borders in 1938

------ Borders of *Reichskommissariat Ukraine (1941–1944)*

Occupied by Germany in 1941

Ukrainian Soviet Socialist Republic (1922–1991)

R e i c h s k o m m i s s a r i a t (1941–1944) U k r a i n e

UKRAINIAN SOVIET SOCIALIST REPUBLIC (1922–1991)

Kyiv

Zhytomyr

Berdychiv

Monastyrok
Hvizdyarnya
Yasnograd
Romanov
Korchivka
Romanovka

0 25 50 km

© 2024 – The Azrieli Foundation

Living Faces of the Dead. A tribute to Malka's murdered family.

To the memory of all my family members and the Jewish people of Romanov who perished at the hands of the Nazis and did not live to tell their stories.

The blood of six million men, women and children cries out for justice. The bloodshed and inhumane sufferings cannot be forgotten. It has to remind us, every day, the human duty of human mercy.

Quiet Sorrows

I was brought to this world not by chance, but, I believe, by destiny. It was a wintry January day in 1931 when my mother was on her way to the hospital by sled; it flipped and ran over my mother, fortunately not causing harm to either my mother or her unborn child. My destiny was to be born, to endure the sufferings that were yet to come.

We lived in a Jewish shtetl called Romanov (now Romaniv) in Ukraine, in the region of Zhitomir and not far from the so-called Jewish capital, Berdichev.[1] My father had left my mother before I was born, and my mother worked out of town, so my mother's family, her aunt and mother, were my caregivers and means of support. It was difficult for my mother to come home during the week because she worked ten kilometres away, as a bookkeeper at the military airport in Romanovka, and transportation was limited. So, she would return occasionally to visit me, usually only coming home for the weekends.

My grandmother Meiti Kantor and my great-aunt Gitl Kantor had come together after great sorrow had stricken them. After my grandmother had been married for twelve years, God had still not given

---

1 In the late nineteenth century, Jews comprised 80 per cent of the population in Berdichev (now Berdychiv). Present-day spelling of the region is Zhytomyr. Romanov was called Dzerzhinsk (Dzerzhynsk) between 1933 and 2003; the author has chosen to use Romanov throughout.

her and my grandfather, Moshe Zeltser, children. My grandmother was told that she would need an operation to correct the problem, and so she was admitted to the hospital. The primitive conditions of the hospital then, in the early 1900s, meant that the success of the operation was not guaranteed. My grandmother was very sensible, and she knew in her heart that she did not need the operation. And so, both my grandparents left the matter of having children entirely in God's hands, praying and believing that someday they would have children.

Finally, they were blessed with two children. First, their son arrived, and they named him Zus. Two years later, a girl was born — my mother, Brindl (Bronia). The joy and happiness in my grandparents' home was short-lived. When my uncle Zus was four and my mother was two, their father died suddenly. My grandmother was left alone with two children, facing many difficulties.

Her sister Gitl had lost her husband and child to illness, so the sisters began to live together so that they could support each other. More troubles fell upon them when their older sister Chava died, leaving six children behind. Later, three of Chava's older boys left for America, where they established themselves as successful businessmen. The rest of the family tried to survive the hard times and famine of the early 1930s, which brought much suffering to our entire community. This was the time when I came into this world.

My early childhood was primarily spent with my grandmother and great-aunt, both older women. I did not have any siblings and felt bored and lonely most of the time. My family was Orthodox, and my great-aunt educated me in Judaism. I spoke Yiddish well, I knew what charity meant, and I developed a great passion for giving help to those who asked for it.

But I was growing up in a home of quiet sorrows; there were no smiles, no songs, no intense happiness or laughter. My early childhood teachers, my great-aunt and grandmother, could not overcome their losses. They would often rekindle memories, pushing themselves further into their world of sorrow.

Malka's Spirituality. Malka's grandmother prays for Malka's life at the gravesite of Rabbi Levi Yitzchok.

In 1937, when I was six, pneumonia struck me severely, affecting both lungs, causing a high fever and putting my life in jeopardy. The doctors, Bitman and Freedman, did all they could to save me, but this was the time of no antibiotics. My chances of dying were very high. My family believed that only God could perform the miracle that was needed so badly. So my grandmother promptly left Romanov for Berdichev to visit the holy site of the grave of the Hasidic master Rabbi Levi Yitzchok of Berditchev. He was devoted entirely to God and to the Jewish community, and his spirit continues to live in all those who know his name. My grandmother arrived at his grave, prayed and gave charity. She promised God that she would sacrifice a lot if He spared my life. She promised to give away all my clothes to poor children, leaving me only what I was born into this world with. She then blessed a penny on the holy grave and brought it to me as a token to guard and restore my life.

As my grandmother had promised, when she returned home, she immediately gave away all my clothes. She borrowed a nightgown for me from our neighbours, who had a six-year-old boy named Lusic Vexelman. When I put on the nightgown, my grandmother wrapped the blessed penny in the folds of the fabric so that I would wear it constantly.

To the astonishment of the doctors, friends and neighbours, the miracle began, and I started showing signs of recovery. In a short time, I was up on my feet. My family was relieved, so happy I was alive. When I was still in bed recuperating, my mother's supervisor, Mr. Danilevitz, came to visit me to witness this rare miracle with his own eyes. He and his family lived in the village Vrublivka, which was about five kilometres from Romanov. He brought me a roll of beautiful heavy linen with a pretty design of red and white for making new clothing. New clothes were made for me, and I did not sense any loss that my old ones were gone.

Little by little, the high fever left me. My energy came back slowly. My great-aunt Gitl gave me the best care she could. She was an excellent cook and made the very best Jewish specialties, but I was an anaemic child who hated any kind of food. I soon started going back to the synagogue with my grandmother and great-aunt Gitl on Shabbos, the Sabbath.

In the fall of 1938, I started school. Despite the fact that I spoke only Yiddish, I was enrolled in the Ukrainian school instead of the Jewish school, the Talmud Torah that was in our synagogue. I was absolutely unprepared, and the first year was very difficult. I practised saying each word, storing the pronunciations in my memory. As the other children wrote on the blackboard, I would go up and try to write also. But my writing would dip downward, causing me embarrassment and concern. Also, we supplied our own pens and the ink for the inkwells and I ruined many pages of paper from the dripping ink, which made me worried and upset. After half a year, I started to show great improvement, and in Grade 2, I finished as an A student.

Like the other students, I walked to and from school in the harshness of winter. Conditions at the school were primitive — as at home, there was no running water, heat or electricity. We had only kerosene lamps.

Though it was tough at the beginning, I have a lot of fond memories of this time. I enjoyed the games in the playground in between classes with my two best friends, Musia Hait and Dora Solovay. I continue to carry their memories with me. Musia Hait had curly blond hair that she wore in two long braids. During the break, she would organize games, and she inspired everyone to enjoy themselves. Her laughter, energy and vitality were so attractive and emanated throughout her being. Nobody knew how unhappy she really was in her heart, that her happiness was only on the outside. Musia told me that her father had left her mother, Shifra, for a gentile village girl, to whom he gave a beautiful shawl he had stolen from Shifra. Shifra ended up in the hospital, suffering from a nervous breakdown. Musia and her brother were cared for by relatives. I felt very sorry for my friend and felt her pain. I felt so empathetic and could relate to her because I did not know my father. I never saw him, never heard from him. I was always filled with the pain of rejection. Musia was strong and smart, and she knew how to run from tragedy to moments of joy.

Dora Solovay was the opposite of Musia. Dora was a quiet girl from a good Jewish family, and we often played at her home. I recall many happy memories playing outside with both my friends and with my uncle Zus's children.

One day, I dropped into the home of my neighbour, Ita Dochovichny, to ask her daughter to play with me in the yard, but the girl was already outside playing with a group of children. I stayed with Ita to watch how she koshered a chicken after bringing it back from the *shoychet*, the butcher who is certified in the proper slaughter of animals so that they are kosher. Ita worked so devotedly, so quickly and so well that I felt drawn to watch her until the end. First, she plucked pin feathers from the chicken and held the chicken above the flames to burn off the remaining feathers, fluff, and to kill any bugs, bacteria and any other impurities. When the chicken was clean, Ita removed the neck veins and innards and dissected the chicken. She salted it and let it rest on a special board to drain, and then she soaked the chicken to take out the salt. After the soaking, the chicken was washed and was ready to be cooked.

Ita also koshered the liver and cleaned the feet to use in chicken soup, as they added great taste. I mentioned to Ita that this chicken would be enough for two dinners. Ita was amazed that at my age, I would have this sense of economy and mentioned it to my aunt Gitl.

Whenever I speak about my neighbours, I recall times that were filled with a great spiritual atmosphere, an atmosphere created through the total devotion of our community to God and to the teachings of our sages, the traditions of our ancestors and family values.

One man who lived in Romanov, called Gershon, was from a well-to-do family. He was so handsome, so presentable, and I can still see his face, his stature, his curly black hair in my mind. Something was very wrong with this man because, for no reason, he would go door to door to beg for food. But everyone in the shtetl was very kind to him. When I would see Gershon from afar, I would run to my aunt Gitl asking for something to give him. I knew she always gave him food, but it made me very happy to give it with my own hands. I would run to meet Gershon before he was in front of our door. He knew me as his admirer and sympathizer.

My community was very religious, and people had strong beliefs that everything comes from God — the blessings and the punishments. People were always trying to please God as best they could, through acts of charity, because of these beliefs. These memories, of giving to community members from the depths of our hearts, still remain very strong and deep.

The History of Romanov. In the shtetl, Malka and her community observe and celebrate Jewish holidays.

Changing Seasons

How many memories I have of spring from my early life! I always looked forward to the arrival of spring, which brings a sense of renewal and reawakening by feeling connected to the cycle of nature. The spring sun energizes us into motion, and trees wake up from a long winter rest, putting on a green coat that pleases the eye with its true beauty. It feels like the world is coming to life.

Spring is also the time of the Purim festival, which commemorates a breathtaking victory of the Jewish people over their enemies. Throughout our history, we have seen miracles, and despite centuries upon centuries of persecution, we have survived and flourished by the grace of God. For Purim, we used to bake *hamantaschen*, a traditional three-cornered pastry filled with poppyseeds. We also sent gifts of food to friends and family in commemoration of the unity and friendship that helped bring about the Purim miracle.

The next spring holiday we celebrated was Passover, an eight-day holiday of biblical origin marking the birth of the Jews as a people over three thousand years ago, when, under the leadership of Moses, they emerged from physical and spiritual slavery in Egypt as a unique nation, devoted to the will of God.

My Shtetl Romanov. Malka's memories of market days, koshering a chicken and making matza.

With Passover came the pleasant sun, fresh spring air and blossoms, and birds sitting on tree branches singing songs that pleased people and expressed their own joy in the spring weather. There was a special place in my shtetl where our community gathered with flour and water, the ingredients needed to bake matza, the unleavened bread eaten on Passover, called in the bible "the bread of affliction." My neighbours and my family would spend a day helping each other bake the matza before the start of the holiday. Everyone participated — men were in charge of making the dough, and women would roll the matza into a round shape to be baked. Once finished, the matza was placed into a special wooden box that was lined with new white linen to make sure that the bread of affliction was kept in the purest state to meet the standards of the holy Passover holiday. When each family was finished baking matza, they would leave a tiny bit of dough to be baked as a treat for the children, who would receive a blessing and the transmission of the beliefs that would be with them for life. There was not one person in our community who did not attend with great pride to the many details required for celebrating those beautiful days on which we worshipped God according to the teachings of our ancestors.

The days before Passover were not only for baking matza, but also for cleaning the house thoroughly. Mothers and grandmothers worked hard to clean, making everything ready to celebrate Passover with pride and enjoyment. Days before Passover, boxes filled with special dishes and plates were taken down to the kitchen from the attic, where they were kept the rest of the year.

Throughout the eight days of Passover, I would see real enjoyment on my neighbours' faces when my family and I went to the synagogue. After the festive season, life would go back to its normal pace, and I would return to school.

As spring changed to summer, I had more fun things to do. My aunt Manya, one of my father's sisters, worked as a teacher in a Jewish school in a town called Yanushpol (now Ivanopil'), not far from

Romanov, and would come visit her parents in the summer. She always showed me love and care. My mother's family made sure I stayed in touch with my paternal grandparents, Mendel and Ruchel Bleinis — Zaida and Babushka to me — and I would visit them regularly, celebrating Shabbos and many holidays with them. I know that I brought some light into their lives as their children had grown and moved away to start their lives in bigger cities, leaving them on their own.

My Zaida and Babushka lived in a big house on a large property. My grandmother had a cow and chicken. I was afraid of the cow, and even of the chicken. In the garden were vegetables and fruit trees — apple, plum and sour cherry, which my grandmother made homemade wine from. Whenever I visited them, my grandmother would ask my Zaida to give me some of the cherries from the wine. The alcohol in those cherries was strong, and two or three of them made me feel drunk! I ate them out of politeness and appreciation for my grandparents.

My grandmother had a passion for helping the poor, lonely and ill, and there was a widow and her son living in their house. The attention and care my grandmother showed toward her tenants was so clear to me and so educational. As a child, I too had the urge to help those in unfortunate circumstances, like Gershon, and give them what they needed. Seeing their faces changing as they experienced the goodness expressed to them was a balm.

The passing of summer brought us closer to autumn and the Jewish New Year, Rosh Hashanah. I can still envision how it felt to observe Yom Kippur after Rosh Hashanah. Yom Kippur was a time of fasting and spirit, of preparing oneself to experience faith in God. We spent the day engaged in prayer, the clearest reflection of the Jewish relationship with God. Prayer in its highest form and at its most sincere level is called "a service of the heart" in the Talmud.

One day before Yom Kippur, every person in the community would apologize and seek forgiveness from friends, relatives and

Malka's Family. Malka spends time with and learns from her paternal grandparents, and loves celebrating her aunt Feiga's wedding.

neighbours to heal any ill feelings that may have arisen during the past year. We spent all of Yom Kippur day in the synagogue, praying and listening to the sound of shofar, which proclaims the coronation of God as King of the Universe, awakening us to repent and return to God.

However, no Jewish holiday meant more to my community than the holy Sabbath. Great care was taken in our shtetl to observe all the rituals of the day. On Thursday and Friday preceding the holy Sabbath, households were preoccupied with the preparation of special meals. Every Thursday, I went with my aunt Gitl to the *shoychet*, who would slaughter a chicken, a goose or a turkey for us. Then my aunt would prepare it according to the kosher laws and cook the most delicious chicken soup with matza balls. By that time, I knew how to kosher a chicken. Baking challah (the traditional braided Sabbath bread) and cooking cholent was a must. Cholent is a stew made of barley, beans, meat, onions and some vegetables that is cooked on very low heat overnight from Friday to Saturday afternoon — and it is the most delicious dish.

Our community placed great emphasis on the tidiness and cleanliness of our homes and in cleaning our bodies before the holy Sabbath. There were no baths, or even running water, in our homes, but there was a communal bath house where we all bathed before the Sabbath. We would then dress with great pride to celebrate the holy Sabbath.

Our Orthodox community had a strong sense of unity. Through charitable donations from Jews who were better off, the elders of our synagogue assisted poorer Jews to celebrate the holy days with equal joy, pride and thanksgiving to God.

With autumn came the return to school. I didn't mind going to school, but it meant that soon winter would begin. I did not enjoy the severely cold winters, which brought hard frosts, high winds and lots of snow. As I mentioned, we did not have heat or lights in the classroom — our fingers would get so cold that we could not hold our pens and the ink would freeze.

And yet, despite the harsh conditions, the winter months would bring some enjoyment. In our shtetl, we celebrated the holiday of Hannukah, which commemorates the dedication of the Temple in Jerusalem that had been defiled by the Greeks but was returned to Jewish hands. I had many nice experiences celebrating Hannukah as a little girl. My grandmother and great-aunt made me a beautiful silk shoulder bag for Hannukah *gelt*, the gift of money children would receive on the holiday. I felt proud as I made the Hannukah rounds to my many relatives, who lovingly waited for me to present their gifts of money. And I saw how happy my relatives were to celebrate, and a similar happiness being expressed by the other families in our shtetl. I shall never forget how I used to look forward to Hannukah. Those were very happy times indeed.

When I recall memories of the better days in my life, my aunt Feiga's wedding is among them. It was a traditional Jewish wedding based on Jewish customs and with lots of joy. Before the wedding, Feiga, my father's sister, was busy preparing for the day. She came from out of town to her parents' home, where she would celebrate this sacred event with family and friends. Her groom, Pinya Rubinstein, was also from Romanov. When she was making her rounds before her wedding day, she took me along, which made me feel special.

As our other relatives arrived — everyone except my father — I felt like an important guest and watched the whole ceremony attentively. I especially loved seeing the bride and groom as they stood under the chuppah, symbolically beginning their life together in a "house" resembling that of Abraham's, the first Jew, whose tent was open on four sides so that travellers would feel comfortable stopping in.

Another memorable lifecycle event that we celebrated in my shtetl was the *bris*, which celebrates the birth of a boy. Family and friends would bake lots of goodies to treat the children who would come from all over town to visit the household with the newborn baby boy. One did not have to be invited to share the joy and happiness, and we would celebrate these events in a communal way.

~

In 1939, I was stricken with pneumonia for the second time. It was as bad as the first time, and my chance of survival was low because the medical options were still limited. My grandmother, without any delay, left once again for the city of Berdichev and travelled to the holy site of the famous Rabbi Levi Yitzchok's grave, where she said all the necessary prayers and prayed on a token coin for me to live and recuperate. As in the first case of my illness, my grandmother gave away all my newly made clothes to the poor children in Romanov and gave charity. In the synagogue, a minyan of ten men wrapped in white prayer shawls added the name Ethel to my Hebrew name of Malka, following the custom of adding a new name for someone who is gravely ill. From then on I was Malka Ethel. The community saw the miracle of my recovery with their own eyes. My mother came home more often to help look after me. The danger passed, and I started to recover and gain strength.

At around this time, news of war shook our town. Five refugee families from Poland arrived in our shtetl, fleeing from the Nazis, who had just invaded their country. The community tried to help the newcomers adjust to their new life with us. I have often wondered how much my community found out from these refugee families about what was happening under the Nazis in Poland and whether this made them more aware of the disaster that was to come.

I think my community denied the truth of the news brought by the five refugee families, which still surprises me to this day. Hitler had already made it clear what he thought of Jews in his speeches, in his book, *Mein Kampf,* and in the Nazi-controlled press: he and his

Nazi followers aimed to convince others that there was a Jewish plot to overthrow humankind and rule the world. This was a leitmotif in the thunderous outpourings of Nazi pseudo-science, falsified history and tortured rhetoric. Of course, there was no "Jewish world plot," but they would invent one — and then the Nazis had only to use it as an excuse to justify their plans of mass murder.

War Breaks Out. Malka and her family take shelter from the bombing and attempt to flee.

War Breaks Out

The year was 1941. Spring changed to summer and brought so much hope, so many sweet dreams and expectations. The colourful flowers in full blossom and the new fruits on our tables awakened our imaginations and filled our souls with the desire for new developments and achievements, to climb the heights of life.

One Sabbath, I went along with my grandmother and great-aunt Gitl to visit their brother, Hill Kantor, my great-uncle. I can still hear the voice of my great-uncle saying how he believed that better times would come, when Jewish people would be allowed to open their own businesses and obtain more freedom — under the Soviet system, all properties and businesses were nationalized, property of the Communist government.

~

I had just graduated Grade 3 in the Ukrainian elementary school when, on June 22, the famous Moscow broadcaster Yuri B. Levitan announced the Nazi attack on the Soviet Union. In this moment, people's dreams were broken, and chaos, panic, disbelief and shock followed.

People began flocking to the Razine railway station near Romanovka, where my mother and uncle Zus worked, to try to escape the Nazis, though getting there was difficult. There were no buses, no cars; on the cobblestone roads, the horse-drawn buggies would bounce to such a degree that the sound made my teeth chatter. If the horses had to move to the edge of the road, which was dirt, the dust would rise, creating blinding clouds. But this did not stop people from deciding to leave before the Nazis came.

My family, too, tried to get to the railway station to take a train to escape the invasion. As we left town in a wagon, I began to feel sick from the motion and was passing out. My family had no choice but to return home. So that is what we did.

The day after the war was announced, the military airport near Romanovka started evacuating people to the east. The military officials moved through Romanov, and my mother, my paternal aunt Manya and I had a chance to say goodbye to all the pilots and military staff that my mother and uncle Zus worked with. My uncle Zus joined the Red Army voluntarily, leaving his wife, Rivka, with their four small children. He did this to protect his homeland. My uncle knew that he was likely to meet his death, but he wanted to protect all of us, and so he put his fears away, suppressing them as if they did not exist.

We also had the chance to get onto the military trucks and get out of Romanov. People were going to Kyiv, the capital of Ukraine, and from there would take a train deeper into the Soviet Union or Asia to escape the Nazi invasion. But as we stood there, saying goodbye, we could not leave. We were not ready — there had been no mental preparation for this moment — so we did not accept the offers to escape.

Days later, our town was badly bombed. It was so scary that everyone began running in panic, trying to avoid death. And so did we. We ran to a friend of my grandmother and great-aunt, Kaly, who shared a house with a family. Kaly was in one room and the family in another tiny room. Kaly was a perfectionist and she kept her room immaculate. She hid us in her cellar, which became filled with people like a barrel is filled with herrings. There was no room to move, but the bombardment shook us each time a bomb hit the ground. Luckily, none fell on Kaly's home, and we all survived.

A few days later, after the aerial bombardment, a special military truck was sent to pick us up, but we were still hiding in the cellar. If we had been home, it is possible the truck would have been filled with my family and all our relatives. I now believe it was not meant to happen; I was not destined to avoid the destruction. Perhaps the truck arrived at the wrong time and at the wrong place. In a way, I feel guilty, because I said no to the previous rides my mother and I had been offered as I could not bear the thought of leaving without my closest relatives — cousins, grandmothers and, especially, my mentor, my great-aunt Gitl. I had never been separated from my family, and I was very scared to lose them. We watched each truck until they all disappeared from sight.

The Nazi Invasion and the Jewish Situation. Malka and her community immediately suffer under the new Nazi regime.

Prelude to Tragedy

The Nazis invaded our town at the beginning of July, bringing with them their plans to destroy the Jewish people, Jewish communities, Jewish culture and Jewish religion. My community was shocked when the Nazis invited the non-Jewish population to a meeting held in a yard by the building where the Gestapo headquarters was set up. There, a high-ranking German officer talked to the crowd in fluent Russian, announcing the end of the Jewish era and the resurrection of Christianity: "The Jewish Mother has died; the Christian Mother is resurrected." I heard these words myself as I stood in the alley between our home and the Gestapo building. I did not see any other Jewish people outside; everyone else must have been staying in their homes.

In my earliest memories, Jews lived in harmony and love with the non-Jewish population in Romanov, respecting each other's differences. After this meeting, the Christian population felt free to express the hidden hatred they must have had for Jews for so many years. From this time on, our lives were forever changed, marked by disappointment, despair and seclusion. We were prohibited from entering public places such as pharmacies, hospitals, stores, markets, schools and workplaces. All Jews, with no exception, had to wear a white armband with a blue Star of David on their left arm, identifying themselves to the Nazis. This would soon help the Nazis carry out their orchestrated annihilation.

One day, Grandmother and I tried to enter a grocery store. We hadn't seen the sign on the door: "Entry is prohibited to dogs and Jews." Fortunately, there were no Germans in the store, but the Ukrainian antisemites there threw us out. The Nazis may well have killed us!

As a child of ten, I witnessed the barbarism and brutality of the German soldiers who would demonstrate their devilish powers by killing Jewish people in the streets. In front of our home, which was next to the Gestapo headquarters, a neighbour from across the street, Nathan Kurtzman, was brutally killed with his eighteen-year-old son, Moshe. How fearful were people who witnessed this terror! But the Nazis took pleasure in it, enjoyed it so much that their laughter and loud screams sounded inhuman. They looked like people but acted as mad beasts, hungry for human flesh. This was only the prelude to the tragedy awaiting the entire Jewish community.

One Saturday, my grandmother and her sister went to visit their brother, Hill, and his wife, Hannah (Chava), and they took me along. We sat at the table, talking, when suddenly two Nazis appeared and screamed at us, "Verfluchte Juden!" (Dirty Jews!) They went to the bedroom, where they broke a mirror and took everything out of the wardrobe. They wrecked the house while we sat in fear and shock. As they were leaving, they found a pail of human waste at the front door and threw the contents at us. Human waste splashed into our faces. And when they left, though we were terrified, we felt lucky that they had not killed or maimed us.

Older women began to tell the young and beautiful women to cover their hair and faces and wear simple and ugly dresses so that they would look less attractive and possibly avoid rape.

Almost all of Romanov were forced to work hard for the Nazis. We did not have running water in the houses, so the adults were forced to carry water from afar to wash the soldiers' clothes and provide drinking water. The Nazis exploited us and used derogatory, hateful, offensive language. The vulgarity of their behaviour was dehumanizing. They laughed hysterically, with wild pleasure, while torturing Jewish people. They had no sympathy or human feelings toward their victims.

By the end of July, the authorities, rude and merciless, forced our community into a small area, a ghetto, guarded by the local police.

Our community was enslaved, living in seclusion, with no human rights, no freedom, no hope, and no way of getting out of this situation, which felt like death. But even then, no one imagined the total destruction of the community, of the Jews as a people.

The First Mass Execution. There is chaos, shock and devastation as Nazi officials and their collaborators plan to murder the Jewish people of Romanov.

The Killing Pits

August 25, 1941. It was early Monday morning. A heavy banging at the door woke us up, along with our fears. Ukrainian police ordered us to get out and be in the centre of the town within half an hour. There was no word about the reason for this order. Adults made different guesses; no one knew what was going on.

As we approached the centre of the town, we saw many others arriving too. My grandmother's cousin, Zlata Baker, lived steps away from the centre of town, so we stopped by her home to see if she and her family were coming. They were still gathering things from around the house because they thought that we might be taken west to work for the Germans. The Baker family had two sons and a sixteen-year-old daughter, Bronia. Bronia had had a terrifying nightmare the night before. She was afraid to tell her parents about it, so she took my mother by the arm and went to the other room to tell her about her disturbing dream. Visibly shaken, she described seeing deep dark pits into which all the people of the community were thrown in, dead and wounded alike.

Soon after, we rushed out of the house and into the street. People had gathered from all over town. Faces expressed fear, anxiety, confusion. Many tried to guess what this was all about, why the whole Jewish community had been ordered here.

The crowds were surrounded by Nazis and Ukrainian police who were heavily armed. The situation did not look hopeful. And to our surprise, those who were unable to walk had been taken out of their homes on stretchers, challenging the thought that people were being gathered for labour. The Nazis and police pointed their machine guns at us, ready to fire if anyone made a move to escape or showed signs of hysteria or panic. People started to realize the situation; the procession started its last journey, a death march. We walked toward the beautiful park located a couple kilometres from the centre of town. The crowd of close to two thousand walked with visible sadness, expressions of disbelief.[2] It was quite a journey, which brought us to the military building located near the remains of a duke's castle that had been built on a manmade island, surrounded by a moat.

Men were rounded up, separated from their families, and then marched deeper into the forest where, previously, pits both massive and deep, had been dug. Women, children and the elderly were forced into rooms in the military building. Crowded in, there was hardly space to stand. Windows were locked. No fresh air; no water; no washrooms. People screamed, fainted, losing their minds; children were scared and restless.

One by one, several groups of Jewish people were taken to slaughter. While we were kept in the building, waiting our turns, the heavy ring of machine gun fire instilled extreme fear and terror in all.

The slaughter of the Jews from the Romanov community continued from early morning until dusk — the sun had faded from our lives forever.

Eventually, mothers with children were let go from the building. Perhaps the murderers were tired from their orgy of death and torture, or perhaps there was no room in the pits for the rest of us, but those who had to remain were slaughtered. We left them, still alive, when we had the chance to run for our lives.

That day, we lost my cousin Bronia and her mother, Zlata; her father, Moshe, who had been killed with the men earlier in the day; my grandmothers on both sides; my young and beautiful aunt Manya

---

2   One source reports the number of Jewish people in Romanov as four thousand.

The World Plot. The Nazi regime uses propaganda to justify killing Jewish people, spreading misinformation and hatred.

Bleinis; and my mother's uncle Hill and aunt Hannah. Many other relatives, fifteen or more, did not come home. I never again saw my uncle Zus's children — my cousins Yakov, Malka, Boruch and Avraham — even though I heard that they had survived this massacre with their mother, Rivka, and two of their aunts. Much later, I found out that they did not survive long — all were murdered in their home.

Bronia's nightmare had been true; I wonder if she told it to her mother. All my life, this is what has haunted me: How did my cousin Bronia die? What did she have to do before she was shot? How long was the torture?

We did not have a chance to say goodbye, or to mourn our losses. We all were frozen with pain. We did not and could not cry.

As we walked away, leaving our loved ones behind to be murdered, the shock everyone felt was palpable, the disbelief visible in everyone's eyes. Soon we were running, from death to the unknown. A heavy rain fell as we struggled to reach our homes. It was rare for the rain to fall so heavily at this time of the year. It was as if the heavens opened to sympathize and share the bitter tears of those who struggled to move away from the scene of death.

There were no words, only tears and speechless terror on our faces when we reached our homes. Sorrow and emptiness. The grave silence was lonely, overwhelming. We didn't know who else had survived because all the survivors were silenced by grief, hidden in dark corners of their homes.

So many in our community did not return home — more than five hundred had been murdered. So many homes emptied by the death of all members of the family. The house where we stayed in the ghetto was now vacant. The owners had been massacred.

Several survivors from the pits told their stories after the war, and many gentiles told the truth of the torture of the Jews that they witnessed, or heard about, from the local collaborators who took part in the butchery. The Nazis and Ukrainian police mercilessly cut hair and beards from old men. They mutilated women's breasts and pulled the golden crown teeth from young and old alike. The victims were ordered to undress, to dance and sing before torture and slaughter and to perform other degrading acts at the command and whim of the killers.

When the massacre was finished, the two mass graves were slightly covered with earth. Some people were still alive — some only wounded, and some went into the graves alive. If anyone had helped, many of those in the graves could have been saved. The graves were moving, three days and three nights. The blood seeped out between the spaces created by the movement of those still alive. A few managed to scramble out of their grave by some miraculous force, to witness the destruction. It had to be seen to be believed what the bloody butchery was. Around the mass graves, one could find human hair, teeth, shoes, eyeglasses, clothes. Villagers came to take clothes, shoes, but no one helped those still alive.

The beautiful trees, tall and mighty, absorbed the screams of the tortured; every leaf on a tree is like an independent eye that keeps the truth of the tragedy forever. I could feel that these trees were crying, sympathizing while guarding the mass graves filled with lives young and innocent, taken so brutally by hate and evil.

Fear of Dying

Every day, I nagged my mother and great-aunt to go into hiding. I was afraid there would be a second death sentence, and I was hysterical, filled with the fear of dying. The picture of death, in my eyes, was so dark and scary that I could hardly stop shaking and crying. I could not accept the losses and total isolation. It was beyond belief. To my great-aunt and to my mother, life had already lost meaning. No meaning in life but me. Only for my sake was there purpose in fighting for survival.

We had been ordered to stay indoors. Each day, we lived in fear that the destruction and massacre would begin again. As time passed, we were starving. I had never known what starvation was, even though I was a poor eater. At night, my great-aunt would risk her life, going out from the house into the garden to look for any greens, anything edible.

Usually, my great-aunt did not see anyone in the streets. But one night, after we had been in the ghetto for a month or two, she saw somebody passing by who told her that one day next week was going to be the total and final destruction of our community. She told me and my mother what she had heard. I panicked and I begged them to take me home and for all of us to hide in our tiny cellar in the kitchen. They agreed that there was nothing to lose, that perhaps we would be lucky and could avoid the massacre.

On Sunday evening, we managed to sneak out of the ghetto and get to our house, which was close by, through the rear window. The cellar was very shallow. If it had been any deeper, it would have been filled with water, as was the case for many other cellars. We spread out a cloth in the cellar and took in the only food we had in our home. It wasn't much, only a bit of water, dry bread and carrots. Behind the cellar door, we placed a pile of wood we had prepared for the fireplace, which we used to cook over. Beyond the wood, we had little room for the three of us, but we managed to twist ourselves and curl up together so that the wood would create the impression that there was no room for anyone to hide.

The kitchen was tiny, and the cellar no bigger — no one could imagine even one person could hide there. The wood took up almost all of the space. It was dark inside, no air, and our chances to survive here were slim. But when one tries to avoid death, any dark hole is acceptable. The fear of dying makes people very strong and resistant. People change in an instant and tolerate whatever they need to in order to survive.

That night was worse than hell. Early in the morning, the police came to our home to search for us. Not finding us in the house, they went to the attic; from the attic they came to the kitchen, opened the door to the cellar and yelled, "Anyone there?" They would have seen the wood behind the cellar door. They did not move any wood and just closed the cellar door.

I don't know how I held myself quiet. My nerves felt tight and in another minute I may have exploded, endangering all of our lives. When the police left our home, we could not stop shaking. Our fear grew when we heard shots from our neighbour's place. A woman and two children, a boy and a girl, shot because they refused to leave. A short while later, we heard shots from the next neighbour's place where a nineteen-year-old, physically and mentally disabled, was kept in a crib in the kitchen where her mother could keep a constant watch over her. Both families were shot in their homes.

The Second Mass Execution: Hiding Begins. Malka, her mother and great-aunt try to escape a horrendous fate.

Even today, I still do not know how the neighbours ended up in their homes. We later found out that the passerby's news was true — the second massacre had been carried out in the forest while policemen killed anyone still hiding in the shtetl.

When I heard the neighbours being shot, I thought about my uncle Zus's four children. Were they still alive? And when I imagined them dead after inhumane torture, fear overwhelmed me and I fell near-unconscious, occasionally screaming hysterically, and constantly shaking. My mother covered my mouth when I screamed, afraid that somebody would hear us.

We stayed in the cellar for two days and two nights. We knew we had to leave the cellar, but where would we go? Not finding any answer, we decided to leave the cellar the next evening. My mother woke me up from my deep sleep to get me out of the cellar, but I could not move. My legs did not have the ability to carry me. It was a temporary paralysis. Both my mother and my great-aunt had to drag me, holding me under the armpits.

We left our home through the bedroom window close to the ground. My mother brought two bags of clothes with us. We first went into the home of one of our neighbours, a shoemaker, whose life with his family had been spared for a while, to serve the Nazis and to teach his trade to a gentile. He knew his destiny, that death to him and his family was imminent. When the shoemaker, Blumental, saw us alive his face expressed wonder. He thought we were dead. He was visibly shaken and so was his wife. They were afraid to have us in their home and told us to leave immediately.

My mother made a quick decision to escape to Korchivka, a village where she once worked as a store manager. She had many friends in the village and was hopeful that somebody would show mercy and kindness.

We took only a few possessions with us because my mother and great-aunt had to physically assist me to walk from Romanov to the village. It was dark outside, no one in the streets; the town reminded us of a cemetery. All the Nazis and police were probably drunk, sleeping like the dead.

Our journey was a struggle. We had to walk on the main road, where in the daytime, somebody could capture and kill us. It was only a few kilometres away, but it took us hours to get to Korchivka.

My mother had a friend, Maria, who was single and lived in a nice house that had a cattle shed. Maria let us stay in the hayloft in her shed. We were so happy to be in the shed and could not have wished for anything better. Two days later, the door of the cattle shed opened and Maria's brother-in-law, a village policeman, appeared and rudely ordered us to get down from the hayloft. He was armed with a rifle. When I saw the rifle, the picture of death appeared before my eyes. I started to shake and scream, begging the policeman to let us go alive, but he was merciless. He said that if we didn't come down from the hayloft, he would throw us down. We knew he was going to kill us. Maria remained in her home, not daring to show her face.

We started our last journey. By this time, I was moving my feet, but was weak and filled with fear. Behind us, the policeman was screaming at us to walk faster to the Romanov police station. Occasionally I stopped crying hysterically, begging him to let us go into the fields. He didn't listen or show any mercy.

Halfway to Romanov, close to the road, was a windmill and a single house where a widow with a nineteen-year-old son lived. This woman knew my family. Volodya, the woman's son, heard my cry begging the policeman to spare my life. He came over to us, grabbed the rifle from the policeman's hands, shot into the air near my ear and said to the policeman, "If you don't force them to the police station, I will." Volodya's mother was screaming, "What are you doing? Don't, don't!" But the son, seemingly possessed with hatred, didn't pay any attention to his mother. I fainted and fell to the ground. My mother picked me up and helped me walk toward Romanov.

When we approached Romanov and had to turn left toward the police station, I made a last effort to go straight, but Volodya screamed, "To the left, dirty Jews!"

At the police station, there were two cells, one for Jewish people and one for Communists. Between the two cells there was some space with a table and chairs for the officers. I continued to scream hysterically. I could not stop myself. The fear of dying overwhelmed me, and I had no self-control. It is a miracle that they didn't kill me to shut me up.

The chief of the police station paid attention to my cries and to me. He took me in his arms, played with my curly black hair and said, "Because of the Communists, such a beautiful young girl should die?" I said, "I don't care about Communists or fascists, I am afraid to die. I want to live. Don't kill me!" He said to me, "Don't cry beautiful girl, tomorrow morning I give you your life." Then the cell door opened and we had to get in.

The cell was tiny. No water, no toilet. Close to the ceiling was a small window for the light to get in during the day. There was no room to sit down. We had to stand on one leg, shifting back and forth. Thirty people of all ages filled this cell — among them, a family from Poland with three children, one of the five families who had come from Poland as refugees in 1939 when the Nazis invaded their country; and an old man of eighty with his daughter and two granddaughters. One granddaughter was twenty years old and one was a baby, just one month old. How tragic when the mother of the baby asked God why He would give her this baby at this time. Sorrow filled the cell. Waiting for death in the morning was torture.

Fear burned in my head and in my heart. I could no longer cry; I had no energy. I had not eaten for a day or more. The baby was crying all night long. People were losing their minds; some fainted and no one could help. We all suffered and felt so helpless. Hell was probably a better place to be than where we were.

Malka Survives and Runs. Malka has no choice but to try and manage on her own.

The morning came and the door of the cell opened. We were ordered to get out and to leave the police station. Hardly able to move after the hellish night, we all managed somehow to get out to the yard of the police station. I am sure that everyone felt that these were the last moments of their lives. Most people remained quiet, sombre statues frozen by fear.

All of a sudden, the chief of police approached me and said, "Go, nice girl." People started to cry, not believing what they had just heard. My great-aunt was crying bitterly, pitying my future life, asking who was going to look after me now. People were asking me to seek retribution on the killers, payment for their lives, if I survived. No one could believe that one of the children was going to survive today's massacre. I myself could not believe my ears that I was free to go.

My mother was speechless. Emerging from her shock, she told me to go to the Gusak family. Yan and his wife, Nelly, were my mother's friends from school, Czech people who were born in Ukraine. Leaving my mother and aunt was the hardest thing for me to do. I thought to myself, *Where am I going? What is my life going to be? Who is going to be my family?*

I was scared. I was full of hurt, but I was the one chosen to survive.

While I was running from the scene of pending death, I smelled food cooking in the houses I passed, onions fried in pork fat. I saw smoke coming out of the chimneys and was thinking how unfair life is to us, the Jewish people. As I envied those with the right to live, tears were running down my face refreshing me, and awakening me from my ordeal.

Eventually, I came to the house of the Gusak family. Nelly and the children were home; the door was unlocked. She was surprised to see me enter the kitchen. I said, "My mother and great-aunt are dead. My mother told me to go to you. Please help me."

In a second, I understood that being a helper might spare me. I quickly started to do some housework, trying to gain favour in Nelly's eyes so that she would keep me there. I washed dishes and took care of the baby. A while later, Nelly told me that my mother's cousin, Dr. Purman, was still living with his family. Their home was only a few houses away from Nelly's. She let me go to see all of them. At their home, I could not open the door. I went to the windows; all were shut. There were no signs of life in this house. I went again to the door, knocking and crying. I was alone outside, scared I would be seen by a Nazi or policeman. Luckily, the doctor saw me through the window and opened the door. I walked in and told them that I had lost my mother and my great-aunt. They cried a little bit, knowing that they too were waiting for death. Dr. Purman, a dentist, was teaching a gentile man to learn the art of dentistry, and then his family would be meeting their own deaths, like all the other Jewish people.

I did not stay long, and when I returned to Nelly's, I began to sweep the floor. I was struggling to get used to what was happening. Suddenly, the door of Nelly's house opened and my mother appeared! I lost my speech and could not move. My mother was out of breath and, for a moment, lost her own ability to speak. She was relieved to see me alive and acting so smart. My mother asked for a dark place to hide, and Nelly showed her the storage room in the back of her kitchen.

After a while, my mother showed us her back, which was covered with blood and dirt. Flesh, blood and clothes mixed together. Then, she told her story: After being taken outside, the prisoners were returned to the cell. Then, one by one, they were taken for torture. My mother was led to a small room, and ordered to lie face down on a table. Two young men beat her heavily with rubber hoses — for being Jewish, for eating chicken, for having golden crowns on some of her teeth, for the pilots she was working with, and for Stalin, the leader of the Soviet Union. Her back was chopped up like mincemeat.

Every prisoner went through these brutal beatings by young men, volunteers, who had come from western Ukraine to take part in the torture of Jews.

In the afternoon, all were taken together from the cell to the out-doors. People could hardly walk. They were led toward the garbage dump, not far from the police station. My great-aunt Gitl could not walk, and she was beaten over the head with a club. She lay on the ground, dying. As my mother neared the place of slaughter, she saw a Polish refugee family, with three children, being killed. As she told the story, my mother's face expressed horror, and she could not keep what she had witnessed to herself. She told us of how people were killed, how inhumanely the murderers behaved. How merciless they were to young and old alike.

The chief of police, Papatchik, was there. He told my mother to tell the policemen that she had a secret hiding place for valuables so she might be taken away from the butchery. My mother was shocked by the screams from the butchery and the mystery of Papatchik's be-haviour. We didn't know this man, and he didn't know us. He was a "butcher" himself. He slaughtered hundreds of people. What had he seen in me? Why had he now turned his attention to my mother? She didn't know but did as he instructed.

My mother had nothing to lose; death was in front of her. She told the policemen about the wealth she had hidden in our home, but the truth is there was nothing of value hidden there. She went with two policemen to the shoemaker's home. The family was scared to death. Two policemen with machine guns were standing there with my mother. She confessed to the police that the chief had suggested that she fabricate this story. One of the two policemen said to my mother, "I will go ask Papatchik if you are lying. If you are, we will butcher you right in this room."

My mother was left, guarded by the other policeman, in the shoe-maker's home, all the time wondering if I had arrived safely at Nelly's. She worried whether I had been accepted by Nelly, and how I was managing without her, since I thought she had been killed and that I was an orphan. If it hadn't been for me, my mother would have continued toward the slaughter. Life did not mean anything to my mother anymore; any meaning had been lost after the first massacre. She was fighting against negative thinking only because of concern for me.

The policeman left to guard my mother was inhumane, and he had all the power. My mother's life was in his hands. And so was my destiny. The time that my mother spent in the shoemaker's home, waiting for the return of the policeman, felt like an eternity. When he returned, he said that Papatchik ordered him to release my mother for the sake of the child with the black curly hair.

I believe that God saved my mother's life because I would not have survived this alone.

Left to Wander

That first night in Nelly's home was a nightmare. Even after all we had been through, the losses did not yet register in our minds, and we continued to think that it might not be true. *This cannot happen in a human world. It must all be a bad dream.*

The next day, as I was doing my chores in the house, the door opened and Nelly's sister, Francesco, entered the home. When she saw me, her face turned red and she was filled with rage. She screamed at Nelly for saving a Jew. She picked me up by the collar of my dress and threw me out into the street. I began shaking from the cold and from fear. I wandered the desolate streets. Like a ghost town, no sounds, and not a person in sight. This scene made me more and more afraid.

Then I thought of my friend Zina Babii, who was a gentile. We had gone to the same school, and she lived not too far from Nelly. But when I showed up at their apartment, Zina's mother showed no compassion for me and would not let me in. I was left to wander the streets again; the absence of sound reminded me about the tragedy, and I cried bitterly. I was constantly thinking that someone would kill me, and I kept wondering about my mother, who was still hidden in the house. I stood behind Nelly's house, waiting, wishing Nelly's sister would leave before I turned into a block of ice. Eventually, I saw the door open, and Francesco walked out.

Fleeing from Nelly's Home. Malka and her mother desperately search for refuge.

Francesco's son, Genadi Sukhyi, was a policeman. He had killed hundreds and hundreds of innocent people, so I remained well hidden from her view, lest she send her son after me. Francesco's daughter, Mila, was thirteen years old. Mila's best friend was a Jewish girl, Esfira Roitman, and at first, Mila's parents took her in when all the Jews were killed, for Mila's sake. After the war, I learned that Genadi had shot and killed Esfira, his sister's best friend. He killed her to eliminate a witness to the horrors he had committed.

When I came back in to Nelly's home, my mother's face was showing deep suffering and pain. Nelly was quiet and looked uncomfortable. That day, we decided to leave Nelly's home.

We waited for the dark of night and then, from Nelly's home, we went further down the road to my mother's friend who lived a little bit outside of the centre of town. We knocked on the door and she answered, looking surprised that we were still alive. She was sympathetic, but she could not take us in for the night. She suggested that we go to the nearby villages or forests. But what could we do right now? In an instant, my mother made a decision to cross the street and open the door of the first house. We heard screaming and laughing, the German language. Nazis. In the small hallway, we found bales of straw for the cattle, so we curled up in the straw in a fetal position for a few hours, the straw poking into us. The situation was extremely dangerous, but we were lucky that no one left the house or saw us. The Nazi soldiers must have been too drunk to move.

This did not weigh down our desire to survive. Early in the morning, we left, running from the danger in town toward the villages, hoping to avoid the Nazis and the Ukrainian police. We hoped that the further we travelled away from town, the further away the Nazis would be. We still worried that antisemitic villagers would threaten our lives.

The Village Yasnograd. As Malka and her mother hide in fields and haylofts, Malka must find food in the village, where she both receives kindness and faces cruelty.

Soon we ended up in a field between Romanov and the village of Yasnograd (now Yasnohorod). We sat in the open field, which was not a safe place. Farmers were digging up beets from the ground. We feared anyone who saw us. In the late afternoon, the farmers left the field and walked back toward the village. No one paid attention to us, though people knew who we were. Only one woman, Yavdokha, remained and invited us to go with her to her home. We told her that we felt lost, lonely and exhausted, filled with fears after such a dangerous night. When we arrived at her home, we could see she lived in poverty. Yavdokha had an eight-year-old girl and lived a very lonely and empty life. She had no relatives, no one to help her through life. Since she was starving, and suffering, she was able to show sensitivity to our suffering, too. She gave us the cattle shed to stay in because we could not stay in her home. However, she could not feed us because there was no food. She suggested that I go begging for bread from the other homes nearby. The thought filled me with fear — what if I came across someone who tried to harm me? Hunger gave me no alternative and pushed me on to accept whatever would happen.

The next questions were, how would I start? What would I tell people? At that moment, God gave me a sense that I never thought I had before. I left Yavdokha's shed and left my mother hidden in the hayloft.

The first person I met was a man. I told him I was Jewish, that my mother was hiding and that I was taking on the role of a mother to my mother, going begging to feed us both. I was in luck that the man was very sympathetic. He gave me a piece of bread and several pancakes. When I had the bread and pancakes in my hand, this little success took away my fear of begging. I was inspired to go on to other houses. They all gave me several pieces of bread, transforming my feelings of despair into feelings of hope. Perhaps there was light at the end of this ordeal.

I came back to Yavdokha's home with my provisions. Not only did I feed my mother, but I also fed Yavdokha and her daughter. This gave me greater confidence and energy. I no longer feared leaving the house and begging again. But Yavdokha was beginning to worry about keeping us hidden. We understood this and appreciated all that she had been able to do for us.

Both my mother and I were exhausted and broken, especially my mother. She had lost all her family — her brother's children, relatives and friends, the community and our Jewish identity — in a matter of days. She was in a strange place without anyone to go to for support, to speak about the pain in her heart. I knew my mother was extremely devastated, but children do not understand circumstances as much as adults. Pain cuts deeper into an older person's heart. This is why I knew, right then, that I would have to keep taking on the role of a mother to my mother.

I was very quick to sense danger and to run. My intuition was sharp. I could easily see the goodness in good people and evil in hateful people.

When we left Yavdokha's home, we found a nearby cattle shed and hid there for two or three days. Then we had to leave and look for a home to warm ourselves, to ask for food, and to look for a toilet. In the villages, there were no toilets at all. Villagers used any convenient place outside.

We repeated this process, going from one cattle shed to another, only daring to stay for a few days at each one. Every so often, I would leave a shed and make my rounds to nearby houses to ask for bread. I would then take the bread back to my mother and stay with her for a couple more days before leaving to look for another place to hide. All this time, none of the owners of the cattle sheds knew we were hiding out on their property.

Near Yavdokha's home was a small village called Sushkevitz Huta. It was closer to Romanov. When we arrived at this new place, we first came to a large house, half of which was completed and occupied, and half of which had no windows and was filled with hay for the cattle. Without the knowledge of the occupants, we entered the unoccupied area of this house. My mother dug deep pits in the hay, and we stayed there for several days. Here, as before, I began making my rounds begging for bread to give us enough energy to fight the hunger, cold and fear.

One day, I entered the other half of the house we had been hiding in. I could see that the woman understood our suffering and had goodness in her heart. I told her that my mother was in the hayloft in the second half of the house. She gave me soup in a clay vessel and I took some to my mother. After going for so long without nourishing food, I felt that this soup was the best I had ever had in my entire life.

One Sunday, while my mother was still hiding, I went to make my rounds. I entered a tiny house, so small that it reminded me of a chicken coop. This neighbour had come to visit with the woman who lived in the house we were hiding in. She was clearly stricken by poverty. On her wall, I saw my own portrait, a photograph, unframed. My heart was pounding, although I was wearing a white kerchief, leaving me unrecognizable. I could not guess why this family would place my portrait on the wall. Was it sympathy for a perished Jewish girl, or was it a child's beauty that attracted the attention of these people? After the destruction of the Jewish community, villagers flocked to Romanov to collect and loot Jewish people's possessions. I did not recognize any other items that used to belong to us. When I returned to my mother and told her about my portrait, she too was puzzled.

We spent very little time in this village. It was far from the forests and we knew we had to move toward the forest, which was the safest place for us. We left the village and went back to Yasnograd. We ended up in a field, where my mother dug a pit for us to stay in. This was not pleasant, but we had no other choice. The roads were nearby and we could not risk being seen. When we left, we went deeper into the village, looking around timidly like scared rabbits, until we found another cattle shed to hide in. The next day, I left my mother in the cattle shed to resume my rounds to find food.

The air was getting colder. At night, we would freeze to such a degree that we could not move our hands or feet. We would knock on doors, crying for help, facing people who either let us in to warm up and stay the night or told us to leave. If we stayed, we would be given a bit of bread in the morning and be on our way to look for another place, in search of food, shelter and compassion.

As we wandered, we came across the Melnichuk family, whose father, Mephody, was coming to Romanov to cut wood for the fireplace. Mephody was limping — one of his feet looked bent. Sometimes his middle son, Anton, who was nine or ten years old, would help his father to perform odd jobs. Mephody was surprised to see us alive. He was helpful and allowed us to hide in the hayloft in the cattle shed, occasionally bringing us food.

Two days later, I had the urge to poke my head out of the darkness and sit up in the hay. Right then, Anton opened the door to the cattle shed. He saw me sitting up in the open. He was startled and stunned to see me, a Jewish girl, still alive. He ran to his mother to tell her that there were Jews hiding in the hayloft. His mother, Vera, came and ordered us to leave immediately. She was afraid that her own child would betray her. Vera and her husband were good people, unable to hurt, kill or hate. After we left, we carried a good impression about them.

We faced daily uncertainty, risks and starvation. We constantly asked ourselves, where do we go now? How do we know who we will find when we knock on a door? It was always possible to meet someone hateful, or a policeman who would not hesitate to kill us. From this shed, we ran out to the neighbouring street to another shed, hiding ourselves again in the hay, trying to regain our composure after being exposed by the Melnichuk's young boy. As always, we needed to find a dark place to calm down, away from anyone, to come to our senses, to focus on our situation.

The next morning, I left my mother to make my usual rounds as a beggar. We were both hungry and exhausted. Some people gave me a slice of bread or a potato; other times, people's actions betrayed the extreme hatred within their souls. When I entered the house of an elderly woman, I told her I was a surviving Jewish girl who was starving, and I begged for mercy, for her to give me something to eat. She showed me the food she had and said, "I have bread and pancakes, but I do not give to dogs or Jews!" In an instant I was out of the house, fearing that she would do something bad to me. Our tragedy did not mean anything to her; she didn't show any sympathy, any humanity. She was not the only person in the village to express hatred toward the Jewish people and support the destruction of the Jewish community. Incidents such as this felt very poisonous in addition to our tragedy. In the future, I avoided this house when I made my rounds. Sometimes we felt hopeless, despondent at having lost trust in people, even though we knew we could not survive without their help.

From Darkness to Light

Each day added more suffering and more obstacles to our struggle to survive. Winter was fast approaching, bringing strong winds, storms and lots of snow. We were not prepared for any of this. We had no warm clothing. Ukraine was known for its harsh winters, the frost coming early and reaching minus twenty or thirty degrees Celsius, weather that would last for several months. Even villagers would suffer from the extreme cold, so our situation was unimaginable. We had to try to stay warm, constantly risking our lives, knocking on doors.

During this time, I opened the Nazarevitz family's door and asked for permission to bring my mother to the house to warm up. Seeing us both almost frozen to death, Christina, the woman of the house, kept us in her home for two or three days, giving us food and her sympathy. She and her handsome husband, Pavlo, had three children — two boys, Tolya and Vanya, and a one-month-old daughter, Nadya. Christina, though overwhelmed with the birth of her daughter, was good-natured, and her smile was something we had not seen for quite some time. After my encounter with the older antisemitic woman, this was a heavenly blessing.

One day, a neighbour approached the house; I could hear the crunching of the snow with each footstep. I immediately took my mother into the next room and we hid under the table. Sensitive and alert to any kind of danger, the fear of dying was constantly with me.

The younger son, Vanya, followed us. I had a bad cough at this time and knew I could not always hold it back. When I felt the need to cough, I would signal to Vanya to beat his toy drums, creating enough noise to hide my cough from the neighbour.

The next day, we had to leave this family, as they felt uncomfortable having us in the house. It was so cold and stormy that we hid in their cattle shed without them knowing. Two days later, we left, struggling to reach the neighbouring house, as the snow was two metres high. Not far off, we saw another Jewish woman who was poorly dressed. She did not approach us; instead, she turned away. There were no other people out in the streets. Everyone stayed indoors.

We reached the tiny house, asking for mercy. Two women, sisters, and a ten-year-old girl lived in the tiny house, which was in poor condition. They invited us inside to warm up. The chimney was blocked to keep the warmth in the house from escaping. This caused a build-up of carbon monoxide, and we all got so sick that our heads felt too heavy to hold up. One of the women understood what was happening and started to use the old villagers' remedies, such as putting cut-up onions on the forehead, eventually bringing us all around. When she opened the door, the entire house immediately filled with cold air, but that brought us back to life. Without a husband to help either of them, they were not properly prepared for the wintertime, and the family was struggling to survive. They did not have enough food or the space for five people. We understood the predicament and had to leave.

Our problem was that no one could keep us for any longer than a day or two. And, the experience with the old antisemitic woman had taken a toll on me. My mother and I both understood very well that the safest place to stay was in somebody's cattle shed, hidden in the hayloft. But because of the bitter cold, we had to look for bigger sheds with more hay to protect us from the high winds and risk of frostbite. My mother was very good at digging holes in the hay to keep us out of the cold winds and drafts.

As we walked out from the sisters' house, not far away we found another shed. The door's latch was on the outside, so we could not keep the door closed after we had entered. This cattle shed, in comparison with others we had stayed in, was roomy, with lots of hay in the hayloft. There was a horse, a cow, a pig, and a line to dry laundry on. It obviously belonged to a well-to-do family.

In the morning, the owner came to feed the cattle and noticed the open door. We heard him call out to his neighbour that thieves must have opened the door, but he was surprised that nothing was taken. When he left, he latched the door on the outside and we were trapped inside. We stayed for three days, until cold and hunger diminished our hope of survival. We knew, instinctively, that the only way to survive was to leave. But how would we get out? I quickly came up with an idea. The roof was made from sheaves of straw, and I told my mother to remove a thatch of straw from the roof. She then pushed me through this opening, and I slid out into the deep snow covering the roof. After the shock of the cold, I regained my senses and went over to the door and unlatched it. My mother came out and we replaced the latch.

We then continued to knock on doors, looking for help. Two households told us to leave. One invited us to stay and warm up. We slept on the floor, which was much better than being in the cattle shed. We were starving but were too timid to ask for food. In the morning, we left this house, and while wandering outside, we started to guess who would be the next to take us in. Usually it was people living in smaller, poorer homes that could share our pain, our losses, and would offer help.

In early 1942, we managed to move from this part of the village to another part. We came to a small house that was more like a chicken coop, in which a widow, Matveika, lived with her sixteen-year-old daughter, Zenka. We figured that this might be "the house" that would offer us mercy because of their own sufferings.

It was nighttime and the house was dark and cold. We introduced ourselves to Matveika and told her we were Jews. We were hungry, cold, shaking and scared, unsure that we would find shelter. As we talked to her about our wandering and suffering, Matveika expressed sympathy and compassion and allowed us to stay in her home and warm up. The next morning, I made my rounds for bread. I brought some bread and shared it with the family. Matveika kept us for days but wasn't able to feed us because she, herself, was starving and living in poverty.

One day, I made my rounds and came across the Shkurateniuk family. When I said I was a surviving Jewish girl, Maria Shkurateniuk called me by name, Musya. I was very surprised, because I had never met Maria before. As it turned out, Maria's husband, Dmytro, was imprisoned as a Communist and had been in the police station when my family and I were brought in from Korchivka by the village policeman. Maria astounded me with her generosity, giving me a bean pie that had been baked over the fireplace. I can barely describe but can still remember my extreme hunger at that moment. I was so happy, and when I came back to Matveika's home with the provisions for the day, I made everyone else happy too.

The winter was severe, with lots of deep snow, and Matveika's tiny house was almost as cold as the outside. Her tiny windows were covered with a thick layer of frost. We had stayed for five or ten days, when one Sunday, Matveika left for a wedding in the village, leaving us with her daughter, Zenka. Matveika came home from the wedding and then left again the next day, on Monday, to continue the celebration.

My mother fasted on Mondays and Thursdays to honour the days the Torah is read aloud, and on this particular Monday my mother sent me to a family to get a piece of bread to break the fast in the evening. I left my mother with Matveika's daughter and went to Vera Melnichuk to ask for food. On the way, I lost one of my galoshes in the deep snow and was very disappointed. I dug into the snow to try and find it, but the snow was too deep and my fingers were frozen.

I went to Vera's home and little by little, I warmed up. As I sat and talked with Vera, we heard the crunching of the snow outside — footsteps were approaching. I instinctively jumped up and ran into Vera's bedroom and hid under the bed. All of a sudden, the door opened and my mother entered with a policeman carrying a rifle. I could hear my mother's breathing, she was hyperventilating and asking in a shaky voice if I was there. Vera said no, even though I was there, hiding under the bed. The policeman left, taking my mother with him.

At that moment, I knew he intended to kill her and that I would never see my mother again. So I jumped out from under the bed and ran outside to join my mother. I yelled, "I am going with you!" The policeman seemed shocked, and he left us outside as he went back into Vera's house to curse her. We stood there, holding hands, waiting for the policeman to come back out and take us to our death. As the seconds passed, I pulled on my mother's arm, saying, "Let's run!"

Across the street was an old cattle shed with its door open. We used this opportunity to get to the cattle shed before the policeman came out of Vera's house. As he did, the owner of the cattle shed also came out of his house, and the policeman asked him if he had seen any fugitive Jews. The shed owner responded that he had not seen anyone and that he had been in his yard a long time. The policeman was left puzzled, wondering how we had disappeared so quickly.

While the owner of the cattle shed was in the yard, we were in the shed shaking, fearing for our destiny and being discovered by the owner. But he did not enter the cattle shed; he only stood at the door. When he closed the door of the shed we started to come to our senses. We needed to think about what to do next. My mother reached out in the darkness, looking for a way to climb to the hayloft. When she reached the hayloft, I was still on the main level with the cattle. She instructed me how to get on the cow and reach up so that she could lift me into the hayloft.

The cattle shed was shabby, and part of the walls opened to the outside, but it was shelter. Then, my mother told me what had happened after I left Matveika's home. Zenka went to see her girlfriends, and a short while later she returned with a village policeman to kill the Jews that her mother was hiding out of compassion.

In the morning, the owner came into the cattle shed. Suddenly, the pitchfork he was using to gather some hay from the loft caught on my mother's coat! Quickly, my mother realized this and grabbed her coat free. But it was quite dangerous, as she could have been impaled with the tines of the pitchfork. We remained there for only two days more, as it would have been impossible to survive the cold and starvation if we stayed any longer.

We left and moved to another part of the village, where we hoped to find solace in someone else's home. In a new area of the village, we came across a Polish Catholic family, an older woman with two daughters and a granddaughter. One of her daughters was disabled, both physically and mentally. This woman was very helpful to us as she knew suffering all too well. We sat near the fireplace with them. She gave us a bit of food.

From time to time, I went out to make my rounds as a beggar. I came across a nice woman named Stepanka. She was a Communist and a very different person, with viewpoints rare in those villages. Stepanka treated me with respect. Knowing I still had my mother with me, she would give me a piece of bread as well as a second one for my mother. I knew Stepanka would keep and hide us, but as a Communist, she too was in danger. But her sympathy and her encouragement meant a lot to me and my mother. We started to believe more in ourselves as people, because of her encouragement. The Polish woman could not keep us long as she was already saddled with her own burdens. So we moved to a nearby cattle shed.

Each day, we continued to struggle. At one point, I decided to go out at night to make my rounds. My mother, fearing for my life, did not want me to go out at night. But I was starving. I meant to visit Stepanka, who lived not far from the cattle shed. But the night was so dark, with no stars in the sky and no light in the windows. The snow

was beginning to melt and the roads were muddy. I lost my sense of
direction and fell into the mud. As I struggled to get out of the slick
mud, I was frightened — what if I were attacked by a dog? This fear
made me forget about my hunger. My main goal was to get out of the
mud and return to the cattle shed to be with my mother. It took me
quite a while to get up and find my way back. When I rejoined my
mother, I was happy. I felt lucky. I would have frozen in the mud if
I was there the whole night. Though my clothes were wet and dirty,
the hay kept me warm. Now I was compelled to go out only in the
daytime to ask for scraps of food.

We suffered not only from cold and starvation, but also from a
massive invasion of lice. We couldn't get rid of them. Being curled up
in the fetal position in the hay to protect ourselves against the freez-
ing temperatures did not give us the freedom to fight the lice. They
could bite us as much as they wanted. Lice was not only our problem,
but also an issue for the whole region.

As the spring of 1942 arrived and the weather showed us mercy,
I started to make more rounds in the village of Yasnograd. Once, I
entered a house and met two men and a woman. When I told them
I was a homeless Jewish child, one of the men threatened to kill me.
While the woman was opposing him, I ran away, ending up behind
somebody's cattle shed. I was running so fast that I was shaking, my
heart pounding, wondering if this man was coming after me. It took
quite awhile for my heart to stop pounding and return to normal.
Then I continued my rounds in the nearby area, for the hunger I felt
was urging me on. Fortunately, after this horrible experience, I returned to my mother with a few pieces of bread. When I told my
mother about my bitter experience with this man, my mother went
into deep shock, so intense that she could not eat the bread that I had
brought to her for a long time.

As the weather warmed, I was yearning to get out of the darkness,
into the light. The forests and the trees were starting to grow foliage,

which would create shelter and hiding places. I was growing impatient of sitting in total darkness and isolation. Every day, starving, I was asking people for food and also hoping to gain some sympathy.

My young and exhausted soul was craving to meet the real people who served God in the true way, who would see, in our survival, God's will. I met people who were talking favourably about Jewish people, expressing religious beliefs in the rebirth of the Jewish nation, about God's mercy in the days to come. Those words inspired me and gave me strength to cope.

When spring was in full bloom, we moved into the grain fields between Yasnograd and Monastyrok. This was our new place, away from darkness, a place leading us in a different direction to a new village where we hoped to meet new people. Even then, when we left the darkness and moved into the light, making our home under the open sky in the field, I was bored and felt like going out to see life in the village and ask for bread. Connecting with others helped me cope with my stress. I would leave my mother as before and make my rounds in the village, which was two kilometres away.

The spring had reached its highest point, and the grains had grown higher. My mother prepared an area of the field as homelike as she could. In between the rows of planted grains, she dug a pit, spread green grass along the bottom and piled dirt into a pillow. This was our bed, which was hidden from view by the height of the plants.

The field was very hot and the air was stale. My mother never complained. She was courageous and could manage in any condition. I remember seeing her holding what I thought was a huge piece of liver. It was, in fact, congealed blood from her monthly flow.

It is difficult to imagine how we survived, starving, hunted and having no possessions at all; no change of underwear; no change of clothing; no blankets; no comb or toothbrush; no paper, no cup to drink from or any item to collect water in. None of the most basic things that people require for survival. Perhaps our ancestral history of persecution enabled us to act creatively in order to survive.

The Righteous

That spring, I decided to try my luck in the next village, Monastyrok. There, I met Lidia Kononchuk, a righteous Christian woman who could see, through the curtain of time, the rebirth of Israel, the gathering of the surviving Jews in the Holy Land. She made my mother and I feel that we were people with a future. She made us believe that there was a purpose in surviving, that one day God would have mercy on the Jewish people and give them the long-awaited Promised Land that was lost to them centuries ago.

Lidia Kononchuk was so poor that she couldn't give me a single grain of bread, but I sensed that she would help hide me and my mother. We went to Lidia's home at night, ensuring that nobody would see us. We couldn't trust anyone. My mother hid in Lidia's attic while I got up before dawn to set off to the neighbouring village, where I would beg for food in exchange for work in people's gardens until dusk. Then I would return home after dark and bring in the "crop" of the day.

Lidia had one daughter, Alexandra, who was seventeen, and two sons, eleven-year-old Anatoly and seven-year-old Nikolai. Because the family was poor, with so little food, Lidia's daughter had to work in Romanov as a housemaid for wealthy people. She seldom came home to see her family.

Lidia was passionate about reading the Holy Bible and read it as often as she could. She mostly read the Prophets to my mother, making us children listen. I remember some of the citations from Ezekiel because they were so convincing, so undeniable. They told of the exile of the House of Israel, the nature of their "trespasses" and the violence committed against them as the Lord "delivered them into the hands of their adversaries" and then, with love, restored their fortunes and led them, as one nation, to their own land.

Lidia kept us in her home for a long time, about one year. Both my mother and I developed a feeling of belonging and being accepted, of having a family. As I didn't have any siblings at this time, eating with the boys from one ceramic bowl, sometimes playing together, burning straw in the open fireplace to create at least a sparkle of light in the room when the winter evenings were so long, is a living memory to me.

∽

One day, the Nazis came from Romanov to Monastyrok to recruit youth for forced labour in Germany. We didn't know this was happening, and we were in the house instead of the attic as usual. Lidia's niece, Verka, knew by then that Lidia was hiding Jews in her home. She knew what consequences her family would face if Jews were found in the house. Panicking, she ran to her aunt to see whether there was a chance for us to escape. But there was no such opportunity. The Nazis were moving from house to house quickly, and the danger was intensifying. They entered Lidia's house, and we could see their boots and spurs from our hiding place under the wooden bed. Then, suddenly, Lidia's seventeen-year-old daughter, Alexandra, appeared — she had just happened to come home that very moment to see her mother! Alexandra gave herself up into the hands of the Nazi officials and, with other young men and women, she was taken to the railway station to be deported to Germany for forced labour. It was a mere coincidence that she came home that day to visit the family, thus saving our lives, as well as those of her family. Had she not come that day, they would have searched the whole house for her, which meant that they would have found us! They would have killed all of us and burned the house to ashes.

What a miracle, what a happy ending! For saving our lives, Alexandra was blessed by the Almighty, who guided her as she managed to run away from the railway station, escaping the forced transport to Germany.

When, in Monastyrok, an Eastern Orthodox woman died, I went to the funeral. I had never witnessed a funeral before, and I always wanted to see more than I had before. The woman's open coffin was placed on a horse-drawn wagon. Family and villagers gathered for this procession. I went with the other children in the procession to the cemetery to witness the burial. After the burial, villagers would go to the family's house to celebrate the life of the deceased by drinking large amounts of alcohol and eating a lot of food. As I was always hungry, I was keen for the opportunity to eat enough, so I joined the other children at the house. First to the table went the adults, eating and drinking until drunk. Then the children went to the second sitting. I was overwhelmed with the occasion to eat as much as I could. Before eating, children would get up and cross themselves while looking across the room to the icons of Mary and Jesus. As a Jewish child, I knew, because of my beliefs, that I could not do the same as the Christian children. However, I could not be sitting while the rest were standing, making it obvious that I was different. My heart was pounding. I stood up and bent down to pull my stockings, which did not need to be pulled up. I had avoided sticking out.

I ate to the fullest, and for a moment I was happy, my hunger sated. After we finished eating, the children again got up, bowed and crossed themselves to the icons, giving thanks to Jesus Christ and his mother, Mary. Again, I had to try to avoid this scenario. I was filled with inner turmoil, wondering if I had become a traitor to my beliefs and religion. As a child, preserving my beliefs along with my Jewish identity was very important to me. I kept wondering if I was unfaithful in God's eyes by attending the Christian funeral.

While I was doing my food rounds, going from door to door, I met the Yakovlev family. I came to appreciate them greatly. The Yakovlev family had special Evangelical beliefs and ties with the Almighty God. They had seven children and taught them all their beliefs. Quite a few times, I had the chance to have meals with the family, and I witnessed how, before the meal, they would kneel down, fold their hands in prayer and thank God for the food and their blessings. After the meal, they again knelt down and prayed, thanking God for the food they had consumed. I did not participate in their prayers, and they never insisted that I should. They respected my beliefs, and that made me feel accepted. I never felt afraid while I spent time with this family. I trusted them and even wanted to see them more often, because I could see the wholesomeness and love in the family. A real connection to the Almighty! As Evangelists, they didn't have a cross in the house, and never crossed themselves while praying to God for sustenance and love.

The family always fed me and gave me a piece of bread for my mother. The more I saw them, the more they were concerned about my survival. They expressed a genuine interest in meeting my mother. Once, my mother came to their home and stayed in the attic for several days. In the evening, my mother would enter the house, as this was the safest time to leave the attic. The family would be reading the Bible, the prophetic teachings, verses from Zechariah about the return of the Jewish people to the Holy Land in the days to come and from Isaiah about redemption. I was especially moved by the words that emphasized that God was with us: "When you pass through water, I will be with you; Through streams, They shall not overwhelm you. When you walk through fire, You shall not be scorched; Through flame, It shall not burn you. For I am the Lord your God. The Holy One of Israel, your Saviour."

While my mother stayed in the attic, I continued to do my rounds. One day, I came upon a house at the end of the village of Monastyrok, closer to the forest. Inside were partisans, fighters against the Nazis, who lived in the forest. They were surprised and glad to see me, a surviving Jewish girl. They were talking about the victory of the Red Army over the Nazis, predicting better times for me in the final victory. They were all drinking vodka and eating bread with cabbage, and they gave me a whole glass of vodka made by the villagers. They convinced me that for the final victory to occur, one had to drink a glass of vodka to the last drop. As I was so eager for the victory, I drank the vodka without any regards for the consequences.

When I returned to the Yakovlev family, I told them and my mother about my encounter with the partisans. I knew I had done something bad, but I explained I had done it for the victory. I was a child, and I thought that if I didn't drink it, the victory would not come. For two days I was critically ill, sick to my stomach. This experience taught me a lesson that I would never repeat. Such a senseless act of solidarity!

After spending the next few days in the attic, we returned to Lidia Kononchuk. She was surprised at what I had done but understood how impatient I was for victory.

My mother almost never left Lidia's attic, sitting for days, weeks, months, in darkness, in total isolation. It amazed me how my mother could be so calm and patient in these conditions. She had a way to look outside, though. She used a tin can with both ends cut out, and by pushing it in between the bales of straw that covered the roof she could see the fields and the village, thus having some contact with the outside world and also giving her a little light.

That winter, the cold was so extreme that the two tiny windows in Lidia's tiny one-room house had such a heavy coat of frost on them that light could not filter in during the daytime. The snow was two metres high and there were no people in the street. All the villagers remained indoors, enjoying their homes.

The Village Monastyrok. Although Malka discovers how to blend in at a Christian funeral, she and her mother are later suspected of being Jews.

We stayed in Lidia's home in secret. At first, not even her sister Alissa, who lived in the house next door, knew about us — although she would see me as I made my daily rounds. However, she did not know where I was staying until her husband came to help Lidia make vodka and discovered us hiding behind the curtain. We felt it was time to leave Lidia's house.

But it was much more difficult to go from door to door with my mother. On one occasion, frozen, hungry and scared, we came to a house at night asking for permission to warm up from the cold. To our surprise, in the same house we met Dr. Purman's daughter, Laura. She was so poorly dressed, shaking from the cold and starvation, expressing disbelief at seeing us alive. We, too, could not believe we were seeing her.

When we struggled to find refuge in somebody's home and could not, we returned at night to Lidia's home. We took Laura with us for a few days. Lidia accepted her. Then Laura left and went to other villages. We remained in Lidia's home.

From the villagers, I found out that Polina Kurtzman had survived. She had lived in Monastyrok for a number of months, knitting shawls in exchange for people keeping her in their cattle sheds. Her younger son, Moshe, and her husband, Nathan, had been killed before the mass executions. Their killings were a prelude to the waiting tragedy. Her sister had perished, and her two older sons were in the Red Army. Perhaps she was trying to survive for the sake of the two older children. When I heard about her survival, I was anxious to meet her and bring her to my mother, to help lift her spirits as much as I could. But no one could tell me where Polina was.

When spring came, I was nagging my mother to get out and enjoy some daylight. By this time, Lidia's sister Alissa was aware that we were hiding next door. My mother was afraid, but one day she went out by herself and went over to Alissa's. While my mother was talking to Alissa, a young man, a stranger, came in, sat on the bench and started to ask my mother questions about who she was, where she was from and what she was doing there. My mother was taken by surprise and because she hesitated and she did not give her answers confidently, the young man suspected she was Jewish. It turned out that he was a German civilian from a neighbouring village. Although he did not have a rifle or a gun, my mother started to sense the danger she was in, that she could be reported by this man, so she told Alissa that she had left her bag in the hallway and wanted to bring it in, leaving Alissa alone with the man. Alissa knew that she would have to divert the German's attention from my mother so that she could escape. I was in the street when my mother burst out of the house, all out of breath. She grabbed my hand and we both ran toward a nearby cattle shed. As we jumped into the shed, we hoped that he would not come in and search for us. The German man came out of Alissa's home, looking for my mother. From the cattle shed, we could hear him asking people if they had seen a Jewish woman. Right away my mother and I hurried to the hayloft and buried ourselves in the hay. He was searching for my mother all along the street, asking people about her.

In the evening, we left the cattle shed and went to the home of the Kovalchuk family. They were very good and generous people. They were well-to-do and had a big house, according to local standards. We asked permission to hide under the bed in the bedroom, and they agreed. While we were under the bed, the same young German man appeared at their home! They fed him and gave him a lot of vodka. Then they suggested that he go to the other houses where some young women lived so he could have some fun. They also felt uncomfortable around him and were happy to get rid of him.

Soon after, my mother and I knew that we had to leave Lidia's home as well as the village of Monastyrok; it was no longer safe. Right after we left, we found out later, a villager informed the police in Romanov that Lidia was hiding Jews. Lidia was arrested and kept in the Romanov prison for several weeks, where she was brutally interrogated before being released. We had all narrowly escaped death.

Belief in the Future

After leaving Lidia's home, we moved to the forest, and from the forest, to the village Gvozdyarnya (now Hvizdyarnya). In Gvozdyarnya, we found shelter in cattle sheds, running from place to place as before. Only I knew where I left my mother when I was making my rounds. For several days, or maybe a week, my mother hid in a hayloft in a house that was half finished. When I met the middle-aged woman who was living in the finished part of her house, I sensed that she was a good human being. She lived alone, with no family, and I think she understood what my mother and I were going through. I checked her out a few times before I told her the truth, that my mother and I hid in the hayloft in the other half of her unfinished house. She did not express any surprise. I told her that I usually never told people where my mother was. At this time, I was probably twelve and a half years old.

The woman agreed to keep us in her hayloft for some time. She lived not far from the forest, and from time to time, I picked up some wood to cook a soup in her yard, made from sorrel and fresh dill that I found in the valleys. We shared all the provisions and also the soup I cooked. This woman didn't have much food and couldn't offer us anything, but having shelter for a week or two was more valuable to us than food. This woman, perhaps because she didn't have any children, was very fond of me, of my courage and ability to put things together. She often told my mother how creative I was, saying that Muska (this was my name in the village) can make something from nothing!

The Village Gvozdyarnya. Malka and her mother meet new helpers and begin to feel hope for their survival.

I was always looking for something new to do or discover, or for new people to meet, because connecting with people always helped me to see a light, to believe in the future. I knew that it might be possible to meet somebody else willing to help us, like Lidia Kononchuk had, but from my bitter life experience, being very careful was always on my mind.

My daily rounds brought me across a nineteen-year-old orphan, Nina Makarchuk. Nina had lost her parents in a strange, tragic way. Both were killed by relatives, leaving Nina and her sister on their own. The Nazis had taken Nina's sister to Germany for forced labour, and she had not returned. Nina was very lonely, filled with loss and pain. When I told her about our situation, she could empathize with our pain and suffering. I told Nina that we had no place to stay, that we hid in different cattle sheds, in bushes, grain fields and in other inhumane shelters. I felt that Nina might be the next Lidia Kononchuk. I asked her whether she would hide my mother and I in her hayloft. I said that we didn't need anything more, only a dark, isolated corner. I promised to share with Nina my daily provisions. She did not hesitate for a moment. She agreed to take us into her home. She was lonely, almost as much as we were, and she needed us as much as we needed her. From then on, we felt united, as a family, and were very careful to keep this private, away from people's eyes.

Nina lived near the collective farm and close to the road that connected villages, taking travellers to bigger roads, and then to bigger cities. It was less safe than the previous hiding place. The village municipal authorities used Nina's home as a centre for villagers to bring their milk to be collected in barrels and taken to Romanov, where it was processed and used by the German army. Every morning from eight to ten, villagers came to Nina's home. My mother remained in the hayloft, but she had to be extra careful and stay as quiet as she could so that no one would find out about our hiding place.

Nina was the only worker to collect milk from the villagers, and after ten o'clock, the collection was finished and Nina's home was a quiet place with no people in sight. Every villager was working in the fields of the collective farm, from where everything was going to support the German army. Very little was left for the hard-working farmers. My mother always remained in the hayloft, where I also spent many hours and many days. At night, we went inside the house and slept in the same room as Nina.

During those spring days, the season would bring rain, lightning and thunder. I was extremely afraid of lightning and thunder because I knew it could kill. My deep-rooted fear was overwhelming. I would look for places to hide and I would close my eyes to avoid seeing lightning, but nothing helped. My mother and Nina explained to me that everything comes from God and people shouldn't fear. I understood this well, but my fears were beyond my control.

I still hold Nina's tolerance and care in my heart, carrying it through my life. She was so understanding and willing to help. Nina was unique.

Little by little, I got to know many people in Gvozdyarnya. Among the memorable people in the village were two Catholic sisters who left an eternal impression on me, although their names are lost to my memory. Middle-aged and single, the sisters lived together in a house very different from where other villagers lived. They had a wooden floor in the kitchen and bedroom, which was rare, almost non-existent in most homes. Usually, villagers lived in a one-room house with floors made from light brown clay, extracted from the ground.

Those sisters had different views about life, about people, about human relations. The polite way in which they spoke and expressed their sympathy to me, a surviving Jewish child, was both promising and therapeutic. They let me know that I was as human as anyone else, a child of God with the same rights in this world as other people. In their opinion, the destruction of the Jews was the result of a long-lasting hatred instilled in people by the church, which was ignorant of the true knowledge of the Christian Holy Bible. Only a few villagers were truly educated in their religious history, and therefore, had a healthy philosophy that made them special in my eyes. Those sisters meant so much to me; they were my friends, they wished me well. They added strength to my exhausted brain and soul and inspired me to believe in my future.

These righteous Christians shared with me messages from the Book of Isaiah, verses about the Lord comforting his people and having compassion for the afflicted, about restoring the survivors of Israel and making us a "light for the nations." I carried these inspiring messages to my mother as something sacred, as the best food my mother hungered for.

The urge to explore new places brought me to a village called Sadky, located about three kilometres from Gvozdyarnya. While I was walking from house to house, I came across people who told me a story about a Jewish woman with a four-year-old girl. The mother's name was Ita Baras, and her young daughter, Bronia. They had been hiding in this village for one year, running, like we were, from one cattle shed to another one. Ita, too, was dealing with the tragedy of the loss of her entire family. When I told my mother that I had heard that Ita died, she was very sorry and she worried most of all about Bronia, the four-year-old orphan who was left in the streets without anyone to care for her. I made attempts to find Bronia, but to no avail.

One day, I went to the other part of Gvozdyarnya, which was located on the other side of the village river. While I was approaching the river, I saw a woman with a bag moving furtively, looking back as if she was running away from danger. When she saw me, she seemed startled and started to move faster. Suddenly, I realized that I had just come across my neighbour Polina Kurtzman, who had lost her entire family and was left alone. When she recognized me, she couldn't believe her own eyes. For a moment, we both were so astounded that we couldn't talk. Then I told her about my mother and the place we hid. To me, meeting a Jew was a dream. Polina was one of the few survivors I brought to where my mother was hiding. Nina didn't mind giving refuge to Polina Kurtzman for a while. And I, as before, was the provider, leaving my mother and Polina and going to other villages to ask for food. Both my mother and Polina were left in Nina's hayloft, hidden and quiet.

～

Time was passing by, bringing the hope of liberation closer and closer. In January 1944, when we heard explosions of bombs or grenades, we knew it meant that the Red Army was pushing the Nazis out of the country.

One day, the retreating German army units were passing by near Nina's home. I was approaching Nina's home and saw several Nazis walking toward Nina's door. I quickly hid in the nearby cornfield and could see her in the yard screaming to the Nazis, "Typhus! Typhus!" In Nina's kitchen, resting near the fireplace, was my mother and Polina Kurtzman, both with bandages on their foreheads because of headaches. When Nina realized how close the Nazis were to her home, she knew there was no time for my mother and Polina to run to the hayloft from the kitchen, so Nina told them to pretend to be ill with typhus. The Nazis were very afraid of this and other contagious illnesses and they turned and ran off. Nina had faced great danger — if the Nazis discovered that she hid Jews, she too would face immediate death. When the Nazis disappeared from our sight, we all felt so relieved and fortunate to have avoided death once more.

Yes, the defeat of the Nazis was coming — there was proof. But I still could not digest it. I still needed more evidence. When I was outside Nina's house, I saw many villagers running toward the farm's warehouses. I wondered what had happened and what was going on there.

As it turned out, people realized that the German army was defeated and gone from the village, so they were going to the warehouses to take all the provisions the German army had kept to themselves.

When the farmers saw me, they told me to bring a bag and take some grains. I ran as fast as I could to Nina for a bag. Then, with the bag in my hands, I returned to the collective farm to take grains to carry to Nina's home as a reward for Nina's kindness to us. I carried as much grain in that bag on my back as I could, probably fifteen or twenty pounds, almost too much for me.

My joy was immeasurable, and yet I felt I was behaving strangely because I didn't know how to use freedom, how to be a free person with a right to live. I constantly was asking, "Are we really free? Are the Nazis gone?" And I felt profoundly thankful to Nina for all she had done for us.

Coming Back from the Wilderness. Malka and her mother return to Romanov and try to rebuild their lives while facing antisemitism and the horrors of their past.

Freedom

My mother and I soon left Gvozdyarnya for Romanov. I cannot recall how I ended up in our shtetl after the liberation of this part of Ukraine. What I do remember is the first days of our life in our town. Almost nothing remained except for memories. Many Jewish homes were completely destroyed. In other Jewish homes, gentiles were living there. Jewish possessions had become the property of those who hated us and had participated in the slaughter of the Jewish people. It was extremely difficult to see this and to accept the unfairness.

Only a handful of Jews came from villages and forests to their empty homes and their town of destruction. None of us knew how to start a new life and how to cope with our losses. But life was demanding. The ones who survived had to start to live a new life. So, little by little, we started to look for places to work and for houses to live in. When the survivors gathered and met each other, everyone expressed their deep pain, a constant reminder of our tragedy.

Adult survivors went to the mass graves to pray for and memorialize their loved ones, and to bear witness. My mother and other survivors took photographs of the mass graves for an everlasting memory, to commemorate those who died and to ensure that those who survived, and who had returned to town after the war, would never forget. On the hill not far from the river, in the Jewish cemetery that had been established since the second half of the eighteenth century, there had been many rare memorials, sculpted into master-pieces from granite and marble. These had all been destroyed by the Nazis and their collaborators. That cemetery, on the southeast side of this once beautiful place, is rarely visited today.

For me, now that the war had moved on, it was time to go to school and continue my education. By this time, I had only completed three grades of elementary school. Now I was placed in a fourth-grade class with eight or nine other children. I was the only Jewish child. I went by the non-Jewish name Maria, hoping to avoid antisemitism. An open, shabby, dirty cattle shed was being used as our Grade 4 class-room. There was no floor; the dirt ground was covered with straw. Barely suitable even for cattle and completely unsuitable for children.

Besides the conditions and lack of books, ink, paper, pencils and other supplies, I was badly harassed as a Jewish child, so different and unwanted by the rest of the children in the class. I was a being that was supposed to have disappeared, supposed to have been killed. Many of the children in the class called me slurs like "Zhyd," a slang for "Jew," and other mean names, threw stones and other objects at me on the way to and from school. They told me repeatedly that I was not supposed to be alive, that my place was in the grave, together with the rest of the dirty and bad Jews. The feeling of not belonging, and not being accepted or understood, made me feel that going to school was worse than going to the grave!

The school was in a village quite a ways from the town, and there was no transportation and no friend to walk with. The way to school was tortuous. I was always wondering what kind of harassment I would face that day. How much would I suffer, how long would this ordeal go on?

Meanwhile, a few more families had returned to Romanov, one of whom was an eighty-year-old Jewish woman, Feiga Nogina, who found out that her only son had not returned from the Red Army. He died in the battlefields, protecting the Fatherland and his loved ones.

Her daughter lived far away in Kyrgyzstan, one of the eastern republics, with her husband and two grown daughters. Her son-in-law was a judge in that city and they lived a good life and had managed to avoid the war, but they were not rushing to bring Feiga to live with them. She didn't have anyone to turn to for solace, for sympathy and help. She literally was in the street, looking for somebody to belong to and to listen to her inner pain. My mother and I remembered very well our lonely days in the wilderness, our efforts to find somebody to feel our pain and help us, so my mother made a quick decision to bring Feiga Nogina into our home.

We soon considered her a member of our family. We tried to be as helpful as we could and make her feel like she belonged. Most of the time, Mrs. Nogina was either inside or outside in the sun, warming her injured leg. I spent a lot of time with Mrs. Nogina, especially because my mother was working in the village of Yasnograd and couldn't come home every night because there was no transportation, and six kilometres to walk to and from work was too much for her.

By this time, I was in Grade 5 at a school in the park not far from the mass graves filled with Jewish victims. The location of the school was a constant reminder of the horrors and hatred. I was again the only Jewish child in the school, and the harassment continued, although to a lesser degree.

I was very lonely, and I felt so different from other children, until a new director came to the school. His name was Bondarchuk, and he was a Ukrainian who had left Romanov and gone to another region of the Soviet Union to avoid the German invasion. He was a Communist. He had respect for Jewish people and sympathized with me and my situation. When the school was preparing a concert, he asked me to sing a Jewish song, thinking it would enrich the program. I had mixed feelings, honoured by his offer but afraid, expecting that other students would react negatively. I turned it down, thinking that nobody would be interested, worried I would be harassed even more.

A few months later, a Jewish family returned to Romanov and settled next to our home. Their older daughter taught Russian language and literature at the school and their younger daughter was in a higher grade in my school. It felt so good to have a Jewish teacher and another Jewish student in the school.

A Bitter Reunion

Among the survivors who returned to Romanov from hiding places in the nearby villages was a man from Poland named Josef Peck whose family had perished in the destruction. He was kind, smart and good-looking, and he offered his hand to my mother and was willing to start a new family with us. But the Red Army mobilized him, and he went to the west as a soldier to continue the fight against the Germans. He kept in touch with us, dreaming to reunite with us abroad, possibly in Austria. We waited for his visa permission, hopeful to leave Romanov for the country he would end up being posted in.

One morning, my mother left our home for work in Yasnograd. While she was walking, she saw a truck stopping in the centre of Romanov, and in it she recognized my so-called father. She pretended that she didn't see him and went to work. I was at school. When I returned home, I passed by the home of my Russian teacher, Chava Rubinstein, and saw her working in the garden. When she saw me, she rushed to tell me the good news: "Musya! Your father came back to you!" I said, "I have no father. What are you talking about?" I ran to my house and put my ear next to the entry door to check whether there was a man in the house. I heard Mrs. Nogina talking to a man. I was afraid to open the door. I didn't want to see him. I went to Nucya, a neighbour, and cried when I told her the news. I didn't want to go home, and I wasn't happy at all. I didn't feel like going to meet my so-called father.

Nucya brought me to my home despite my fears. When we entered the house, the so-called father tried to give me a kiss, which was too bitter to swallow. I was filled with the pain of abandonment, with bad memories about his total absence in my life. It was too much for me, especially at that time. I needed a peaceful home to escape from the school harassment, which to me meant the continuation of the war. I needed more good friends, more kind people, to create for me a new and better world. The father who left me without any regret fifteen years earlier, even before I was born, was a constant reminder of the pain I felt in childhood while watching other fathers show love and affection to their children.

The return of the so-called father was a great sensation to the people of the town, and to the people of the villages where I had survived. People, both Jewish and gentile, were saying that this was a rare miracle that brought our family together. People didn't know that he had had a wife and two children. His other family had perished, and he was left alone. When he didn't have a place to go, he took a chance by coming back to Romanov. I remembered my mother's story from long ago, how the so-called father had come once with his wife to Romanov, took her to my mother's home and introduced the woman as his cousin. The woman was pregnant. Both of them admired the beauty of the child my mother was holding in her arms — me — and then left forever, without any more contact. I could not forget this, and never felt I had a father somewhere in the world. He came for his own sake, not for mine.

By this time, my mother had bought the house we lived in from a survivor who had decided to leave Romanov. My mother had a good job as a store manager. She was involved in the life of the small Jewish community. She was very active in hunting down Ukrainian and Polish police collaborators. She did not ask me how I felt about accepting back her husband, my so-called father, and didn't pay attention to my pain.

My life turned into another nightmare. He, instead of looking for ways to earn my trust and love, started to abuse me mentally and physically. He beat me with the end of his metal belt buckle, hitting me, hurting me. He told me I was nothing. The abuse was so harsh, almost unbearable. I constantly feared for my life. The hardships I faced at school cut my heart open. And then, I had to face going home. Survivors would hide me in their homes, guarding me, shutting the windows from outside with wooden shutters, so that he wouldn't break the glass of the window and take me for punishment. The reason for being punished was not known to anyone, including me. Nor was it known to the so-called father. My mother was afraid of him and was unable to protect me. She was also verbally abused by him. She could not stand up to him nor could she defend me against him. Sometimes, she just cried, sobbing as he threatened to kill me. Most of the time, she did nothing.

One day, when I came home from school, my mother was crying, and on the porch, I saw that a bunch of my best clothes had been chopped into pieces with an axe. I could not believe my eyes. I cried and was afraid he would chop me up, too. These were clothes that my mother had bought for me in the bazaar before he came back to us. There was nothing he brought me or bought. He made my mother and I his slaves. I was in my teenage years and by then I had school friends. I wanted to go with them to the cinema, to a dance, or wherever my friends went. He never let me go, keeping me home, where I would cry all night in fear of him.

A few months later, he decided that he and my mother would leave Romanov for a whole year and go to Tashkent, where two of his sisters lived. I was left with Mrs. Nogina in one room, and the second room was rented to a widow with a fifteen-year-old boy.

That winter, when we used the fireplace to heat up the house, it would take a long time until the wood started burning. The walls of the house were so damp that water would drip down the walls to the floor. The roof of the house was so old that the rain leaked through, causing puddles in our home. The conditions were a real misery.

I was not prepared for winter. The fur coat my mother bought me after returning to Romanov was taken by my father to Tashkent along with my mother. I felt rejected by my mother, leaving for Tashkent and taking all the warm clothes. The stress and lack of proper clothing brought me a strange illness that wasn't easy for a doctor to diagnose. Under my left armpit, I detected two small pink spots covered by a barely visible rash. The pain made me suffer so much that from time to time I felt like giving up. I thought, *I'm going to die.* Mrs. Nogina saw how much I was suffering and spoke to a few women in the village about it. They came to see me and brought oats to apply to the rash. It was painful and felt uncomfortable, but it helped. To this day, I carry the memory and sensations of that pain.

My mother was writing me letters from Tashkent, and one day she sent me good news. She had given birth to a baby boy. I was very happy to have a sibling. I was alone before the war, and a new soul in the family meant the whole world to me.

When my brother, Marik, was five months old, my parents came back from Tashkent. I was glad to see my mother and brother, but not my so-called father, because I was still afraid of him and didn't feel at ease in my own home.

Before my family returned from Uzbekistan, I managed to finish all the work in the big vegetable garden in the yard around the house. I had done all the work in a primitive way, with manual tools, and I didn't have any help. Before school, I would work for an hour or two in the garden, and after school, I would continue my hard work around the house.

My garden turned out to be so nice that villagers from Yasnograd and Monastyrok, when coming to Romanov's farmer's market, would pass by my house and drop in for a drink of water, complimenting me on the beauty of the garden and making me feel like a true farmer. They said they thought that Jewish people didn't like farming and didn't know how to work in the fields; they assumed we were mostly interested in science and business. Nobody had taught me how to farm. I was always attracted to both the beauty and mystery of nature, puzzled by all its hidden knowledge. Closely observing blossoms, different colours and nuances in the delicate flowers, would make me very happy. It would take me away from casual, everyday life to something sacred, to higher energies and powers that create the beauty in this world. I was also interested in showing the villagers that Jewish people were able to work in the garden, producing the same as them and other farmers.

~

I prayed for the time when school would come to an end and only be a memory to me. I wished to graduate high school and move to a big city to obtain a university education. My dream was brutally interrupted by my so-called father who, after Grade 7, compelled me to be a bookkeeper and work in a bank. He did not ask me whether I liked it, whether I was able to do this job and count numbers. He just placed me in a small bank in our town, which was located in a vacant home with primitive conditions. And here I was, a student, learning from the others the art of banking, and learning while I worked how to do all that was needed for my job.

For about two weeks, the so-called father would kick me out of the house, following me with a club in his hands, forcing me to obey him, calling me names and constantly saying that I didn't understand anything. With the help of several bank workers and some neighbours, he was persuaded that this was not right to do to a child, and that I should go to school because I wished to do so. I continued my high school education thanks to these good people.

In the meantime, my mother gave birth to another child, also a boy, named Roman. My love for the children helped to heal the wounds inflicted by my father. But my brothers were not spared his brutal beatings either. When they were aged two or three, he began to abuse them as well. One day, he beat his older son so badly that he collapsed on the ground and could not get up.

I often cried out to God, asking for help when the hardships became so harsh and unbearable, sometimes complaining for the destiny God had prescribed me. In my heart, I questioned why a good person, especially a child, should be punished by God. Then, I would take myself back in my mind to the police station, where I was on the verge of death, when my people were all taken to slaughter. I was destined to survive and to see the light of life. The exceptional goodness of God to me, I always carry in my soul.

Even after I left home, I spent a lot of time thinking about my sad past, about the sufferings in my own family. Those sufferings left scars on my heart. The reader of my story might wonder how a mother could leave a child who had been so protective and caring. I took the absolute responsibility to be a mother to my mother, at the hardest times in my mother's life. Though I was a child, I understood my mother's heavy losses. Neither of us would have survived the war if we hadn't been together.

I never doubted my mother's love for me, but my mother had made a terrible mistake reuniting and marrying, for the second time, a man who was not right for her in the first place. My grandmother had been against my mother's choice initially. The man she married had warned my grandmother, "If your daughter won't be mine, she won't be yours!" A statement that did not promise a good future.

After the war, my mother transformed from a dependent child to a courageous woman who successfully hunted Polish and Ukrainian police for crimes committed against Jewish people. My mother was hard-working and independent. I could not understand why she took my so-called father back — she did not need him for support. She had a home, a steady job. Why? It was hard for me to love her after my father's return because she did not understand my feelings. We only visited each other occasionally. During the war, I took care of her. I was a mother to my mother. Somehow, she could not be a mother in the way of caring for me and protecting me.

Leaving Home

In 1950, I graduated high school and left Romanov for the big city of Zhitomir. One of my high school teachers in Romanov, who had taught us Russian language and Russian literature, had lived in Zhitomir and had graduated from the Ivan Franko State University. Her uncle was dean of the Russian faculty. She contacted her uncle and suggested that he accept both me and my friend Galina Bondarchuk into the university. She knew we would become good teachers. I was very fortunate because Jews were often not accepted into a university, as unofficial quotas limited the number of Jews allowed to enroll.

In Zhitomir, Galina and I rented a space in a one-room home from a family, not far from the university. We shared one narrow pullout bed. The rent was very expensive for us, and the bed was very uncomfortable, but it was wonderful to be learning, and I could breathe again, safe and far away from my father's abuse.

Being at university was a most wonderful experience. How I loved learning! In the evenings, after classes, Galina and I would often go out to the pedestrian boulevard lined with trees and benches where families and single people gathered. It was there that I met my husband, Efim (Efraim) Pischanitsky, who was an officer in the Soviet army. He worked in military aviation, maintaining and servicing the planes for their missions. For Efim, it was love at first sight. He was madly in love with me. He was so handsome, but I wasn't too sure about my feelings for him at the beginning. I did not believe in myself. I had no self-confidence.

At that time, I had only one dress. When I washed it, I would sit in my nightie while it dried in front of the fireplace. When I wore it, it was so beautifully designed that people thought I was wealthy, which I was not!

Efim and I married in 1953, even though I still had another half year at university before I would graduate. We registered our marriage at the government offices and had a small wedding celebration at his parents' home in Korosten. There was no chuppah. My mother came with one of my brothers. In those days, there was no such thing as a honeymoon. After we were married, we rented a room together, where we stayed until I graduated in 1954 with a high school teacher's diploma in Russian and Ukrainian literature from the Faculty of Languages.

Our first child was born on October 4, 1954. We named her Galina after my great-aunt Gitl. It was not acceptable to use names of Jewish origin in the U S S R. She would have been ostracized.

Life for most people was very difficult after the war — finding shelter and adequate food was a struggle. The army paid my husband a modest income, so we were later able to rent a bigger room, but the rent used up most of our money. The bathroom was still outside, and there was no running water. As a new mother, my teaching opportunities were limited, especially with a little baby. Hiring a babysitter was complicated in Ukraine and very costly. At that time, my husband was the only provider bringing in some money. I was limited to a great degree by my baby, so that first year, I tried to take on some substitute teaching positions. But later, I had the chance to get a full-time job in a school and was fortunate to have found a kind woman to help look after Galina.

I was very happy. I had wanted to have children. My feelings about having a real child, my own child, were overwhelmingly positive. I had been so devoted to my mother. During the war, she had been my first child, and I, her mother. I would bring anything that was in my hands to feed my mother so she could survive. But now, I had to learn how to be a mother to my own child. A baby changes your life. You have such a feeling of love inside of you. It does not matter if you are poor, or where you are. There are no words to truly express that feeling of love for your child.

My second daughter, Inna, was born on May 29, 1959. Galina was almost five when her sister was born. Taking care of Inna and working was a bit easier because I had a nanny helping me. Inna was named in honour of my husband's grandfather Yona, following the Jewish tradition of naming a newborn for someone who has passed on.

After I was married, we seldom saw my mother. My parents had moved to Tashkent to be closer to my father's side of the family. In 1963, when my husband left the army after seventeen years of service, we decided to move to Tashkent so I could be closer to my mother. We lived there for three years. It was like a new start, and my mother was very generous as we settled in. It was so nice to have our own apartment on the third floor of a building. Efim found a job working at the civil airport because of his aviation experience, and I found a job teaching Russian literature to high school students at a school nearby.

I taught very methodically and took my responsibilities very seriously. I loved teaching. I loved the Russian classics, especially books by Alexander Pushkin and Mikhail Lermontov, among other Russian writers and poets. Teaching about them was a delight. I was born to be a teacher!

~

On April 26, 1966, a massive earthquake hit Tashkent, followed by many aftershocks. Due to the destruction, we were given the opportunity to relocate to another part of the Soviet Union. We decided to move to Western Ukraine, to Uzhgorod (Uzhhorod). The government was supposed to help us find employment because we had been displaced by the earthquake, but it was very challenging. I was able to find a position teaching Russian language and literature at a high school. There were some Jewish students and teachers, but it was difficult teaching there because antisemitism was on the rise. Jews were hated by many.

For many Jews in the USSR, it was difficult to live a Jewish life. I had been raised in a kosher home until the war, and then we survived however we could during the war and afterward. The Soviets turned the beautiful pre-war synagogue in Uzhgorod into a concert hall, for orchestral music. On high holidays in Uzhgorod, we met other Jewish people in a house hidden in an alley, with lookouts at each end of the street because we were not allowed to practise our religion under the Soviet regime.

Some years later, there was an agreement between Israel and the Soviet Union to facilitate Jewish immigration to Israel. There were only about 10,000 visas issued to Jewish citizens in the 1960s, but between 1970 and 1988, 291,000 visas were issued, approximately 165,000 for Israel. The departure of Soviet citizens who were Jewish seemed to further inflame antisemitism. Jews still had little opportunity to move into leadership positions. They were excluded from meetings and not kept up to date as other non-Jewish employees were. Sometimes the antisemitism was subtle, but often it was not. When people of other nationalities left the Soviet Union, no one was angry, but when Jewish people started to leave, it became very political, very antisemitic and personal. Although we were all Soviet citizens, Jews were despised for being "traitors" if they left. It was becoming a very dangerous life in the USSR for Jews, even though we had suffered so much during the war.

We didn't have any visas. We could not leave. In 1971, my mother, my older brother and his wife left for Israel, where they lived for several years. In 1972, my younger brother, Roman, left for Vienna with his non-Jewish Russian wife.

But as my family was leaving, we were left behind in the Soviet Union. I felt there was no future for us in Ukraine. We could only get visas for Israel. My husband, Efim, had mixed feelings about leaving the USSR. He was a member of the Communist Party and his older brother was a colonel in the Soviet army (ironically, many years later he moved with his family to San Francisco). In those days, you had to list the names of all your relatives, both abroad and in the USSR, to obtain a visa. Listing my brother-in-law on an application would have compromised his position and career opportunities. By this time, there was a rift in our marriage, and we decided to part ways. We eventually saved enough money to purchase exit visas for myself and the children.

I left the USSR with my daughters in May 1975, arriving in Vienna shortly before Inna turned sixteen years old. By this time, my mother had moved from Israel to Vienna to reunite with my younger brother and his family. My older brother had left Israel and moved to Vancouver, Canada. Because there was no close family in Israel at that time, we decided to go to Canada. We left Vienna after a few weeks and spent six months just outside of Rome while waiting for our Canadian visas.

We ended up in Canada even though everything had been prepared for us to go to Israel. We landed in Vancouver in December 1975, where my older brother lived and was our guarantor. Once we settled in Canada, Efim came to visit us twice and was in regular contact with Inna and Galina.

Life was not easy for immigrant families, especially ours because we did not know any English. I attended English classes at school with my older daughter, Galina. Inna went to new Canadian classes full-time for six months before enrolling in high school. I was very enthusiastic about finding a job and working but I had a difficult time adjusting. I was at a disadvantage looking for work as a teacher because of my limited English-language proficiency and lack of Canadian work experience and qualifications. I did some odd jobs and volunteered with seniors at the Louis Brier Home and Hospital, gradually improving my English skills.

My daughter Inna graduated from Eric Hamber Secondary School in 1978 when she was eighteen. She attended the University of British Columbia and earned her degree in social work. She worked for several years at the Shaughnessy Hospital and Vancouver General Hospital before travelling to New York, where she earned a master's degree in social work from Yeshiva University. In 1985, Inna was the first director of the L'Chaim Adult Day Centre, which is a culturally Jewish day program for seniors. It is a wonderful place for seniors to socialize, share lunch, exercise and go on day trips. I attend three days each week. I am blessed to have Inna and her family living close by in Vancouver. I stay with her often during the week.

My daughter Galina graduated from art college in Uzhgorod and retrained in Vancouver as a certified orthodontic assistant. She works in a busy orthodontic office. She comes and stays with me whenever possible on weekends.

I am blessed with four grandchildren — Effie and Karin are Galina's daughters, and Sophie and Solomon are Inna's children. Education has always been important to me and I am very proud they have all graduated from university. They know my story, all of it.

After arriving in Canada, it was important for me to reconnect with my Jewish roots, considering how impossible it had been to embrace Judaism while living in the Soviet Union. I found a welcoming spiritual home at Chabad Lubavitch in Vancouver. It was a bonus that many of the Lubavitch members spoke Yiddish. Finding a place to speak Yiddish was wonderful for me because in the beginning my English was very poor.

I have kept a kosher home in Canada for many years and I raised my children in a Jewish home. I read the Torah every Saturday. Torah is a teacher. Torah is a doctor. I believe that if we read the Torah, we will obtain wisdom from it that we can use in everyday life. We will make fewer mistakes in life. God is in charge of my life and God has saved me many times from the dangers that have surrounded me.

I was able to visit Israel, the Holy Land, nine times. Each time, it was like coming home. The first time was in 1983 and the second when Galina was married in Israel in 1986. The first time I saw young Israeli soldiers with rifles I was so overwhelmed I couldn't stop crying. I cannot explain the depth of feelings I had then. There are no words. Only looking at my face, you might have understood. Israel is a holy country. God is there. It is His home and mine. My ancestors are there. My spiritual home is there.

Righteous Gentiles. Malka honours the non-Jewish women who risked their lives to help her and her mother survive.

Gratitude

My mother never forgot the goodness and courage of the righteous Christians, and she inspired me to remember them always. My mother was very generous and knew how to express gratitude to those who had saved us. I have passed on to my own children the importance of gratitude, and the love I still feel toward those who helped my mother and I survive. In the 1990s, I documented my story of survival at Yad Vashem and had Lidia Kononchuk, her daughter, Alexandra Didkovskaya, and Nina Makarchuk recognized by Yad Vashem as Righteous Among the Nations.

After I moved to Canada, I stayed in touch with Lidia Kononchuk. With the help of our relatives in Kyiv, Lidia's children gained employment and obtained permission to relocate to Kyiv. In general, citizens of the USSR could travel for work or pleasure but to change your residence from one city to another was very complicated, requiring permission from the government. Lidia's children were able to leave the village of Monastyrok, coming back occasionally to visit their mother. Lidia passed away in 1985. I kept in contact with her children and then her grandchildren, often exchanging gifts.

Nina Makarchuk, after the war, married a kind man who had lost both his legs due to an illness in his childhood. The man had practical wisdom and was prudent in every aspect of life. They had nine children. My husband and I, with the help of my mother, helped Nina to educate two of her children, Galina and Zoya, by paying for them to go to college. Galina lived with us for three years when we were living in Tashkent, and then moved with us to West Ukraine, to Uzhgorod, until she graduated. Zoya then lived with us in Uzhgorod, until she graduated as well. When Nina's daughters lived in our home, we paid all expenses, hoping that the two educated children would help the rest to move from the village to the larger cities. Now, only three of Nina's nine children live in the village Gvozdyarnya. After Nina passed away in 1987, I stayed in touch with her children.

Before I left Ukraine for Canada, my family and I used to visit Lidia and Nina in their villages. Villagers would gather around us, complimenting me for not forgetting those who risked their lives in saving Jews from slaughter.

On my way to Gvozdyarnya and Monastyrok we had to pass by the village Yasnograd, where usually we stopped for a rest. People would gather around me, asking questions and telling stories.

One story amazed me. Zenka, the widow Matveika's daughter, left Yasnograd for a big city where she married and had two children. One day, her husband took the two children for a ride in their truck. There was an accident and the truck rolled upside down, killing all three of them. The villagers concluded that Zenka was punished by God for putting me and my mother into the policeman's hands for slaughter.

When we arrived in Gvozdyarnya, Nina Makarchuk told us a similar story about a hater of Jews. During the destruction of Jewish people, villagers took Jewish possessions. One of the villagers had picked up a big piece of parchment of the Holy Torah, brought it home and defecated on the Holy Writings, showing to most of the villagers her uncontrollable hatred of Jews. After the war, this woman was paralyzed and was absolutely immobile. Nina told us that the villagers concluded that God punished this woman for crimes against His holiness, for the hatred and evil feelings toward His chosen people.

It is my duty, as it is for many other survivors, to tell the world the truth about the moral corruption of the twentieth century, of the torture and pain inflicted on innocent people for the reason of being different, being Jewish.

Talking about my experiences to various groups and individuals helps me to reduce grief and mental distress. People ask many questions, among which is a common one: "Did you forgive; can you forgive; are you angry?"

I never forgave; I'm not forgiving; and I never will forgive those who took innocent lives.

I Was the Mother to My Mother. Created with artist Linda Dayan Frimer in 1998, this was the first painting Malka conceptualized to tell her story. The photo at the bottom of the work is one she brought from Ukraine, showing the mass graves in Romanov.

Epilogue: My Childhood Through Art

After a trip to Israel with a group of Russian Holocaust survivors, I started to get involved with the Child Survivor Group through the Vancouver Holocaust Education Centre (VHEC). We were and are a family. We have walked in each other's shoes. We all have stories to share and it helps to be among other child survivors, united in the memory of childhood pain and loss. When we share our stories, we are believed and understood. Together, we also share news of our families, world events, names of good books, things to do. We are a strong community. It too is home.

In this group, I began to share pieces of my early life. My experiences, the means I used to survive, seemed very different from the others. I ask myself — how did I survive? A pit? A trench in a field? Sleeping beneath the standing grain? Hiding in haystacks? I brought materials to the meetings, stories I had written, photos, items from Israel.

In 1997, Linda Dayan Frimer, a well-known Vancouver artist, came to the Vancouver Child Holocaust Survivor Hanukkah luncheon. She told us that she wanted to gather a group of survivors to work on an art project called Gesher (meaning a "bridge," to connect the past to the present). It was an open invitation to survivors who had been in camps and who had been in hiding. I told her that I was not a painter or an artist but I wanted to join her project. She reassured me that I didn't need to be an artist to join. About twenty of us child survivors gathered at the Louis Brier once or twice a month. We shared stories with one another and illustrated the themes on a tapestry. Working with Linda and the group on The Gesher Project inspired me to create and conceptualize, over a span of two decades, sketches, then, working with various artists, paintings to tell my story of survival in and around Romanov during the war.

In 2019, the World Federation of Jewish Child Survivors of the Holocaust and Their Descendants held their annual gathering in Vancouver for the very first time. It has been held all over the world, including Berlin, Amsterdam, Prague, Jerusalem, Warsaw and many cities in the United States. It brings survivors and their descendants together to share their experiences, to learn from one another, and to celebrate their resilience as a strong Jewish community. Nina Krieger, Executive Director of the VHEC, spoke with the co-chairs of this event, Dr. Robert Krell and Marie Doduck, and they felt my artwork could have its premiere at this important gathering. I worked with Wendy Oberlander and Adele Rich as well as staff from the VHEC to bring my art exhibit to the Sheraton Vancouver Wall Centre.

Just prior to the World Federation meeting, I was sick with severe influenza that resulted in respiratory failure and admission to the Vancouver General Hospital ICU. It was uncertain whether I would survive, but I did — it was a true miracle. God took care of me. Again.

When I left the hospital, my family took turns taking care of me. They all came and supported me throughout my time at the Federation meeting where my paintings and story were shown. It was very emotional for me. There, almost five hundred survivors and their families attended the gathering and were able to see my exhibition, titled *Romanov: A Vanished Shtetl — A Living Monument in Art and Words*. I had created nineteen pieces of art; each panel was part of my story. As noted in the exhibit catalogue, "…this exhibition fulfills the central Jewish obligation, *zachor*, to remember."

∼

Departed. Mass grave of the murdered Jews of Romanov, including many of Malka's relatives.

The isolation during the first few years of the worldwide COVID pandemic did not affect me as much as it affected others because of all I went through during the war. I felt prepared for everything that one could possibly imagine would and did happen.

People have told me I am a force to be reckoned with. I believe wholeheartedly in the importance of education. I have tried all of my life to be kind, to help people, to respond to their questions and to help them live happier lives. With education, there will be less suffering in the world. Education is crucial. Knowledge opens our eyes. It helps us find ourselves. This is not an easy world. I cannot close my eyes without seeing and remembering all that I went through.

I have two main thoughts about the world we live in: One, when you meet someone, you always get an instant impression, which may or may not be true to who that person really is. They can pretend to be one way when they are another. I was lucky because even as a young child, I could see the real person. Two, we live in a very complex world. We add to it and we take from it. If you study the prophetic teachings, your eyes will be opened. God created us to build this world.

The message I want to leave with readers is this: I feel and deeply believe that God is in charge. God did not create people to murder other people. Don't look for the differences in someone, for we are more alike than we are different. We come to the world not by chance but by destiny. We were created not only by our parents, but by God. We must constantly add goodness to the world. We are not here to add hatred to the world, but instead, to bring love. I love people and feel a deep love for humankind.

Photographs

1   Malka's maternal grandmother, Meiti Kantor (left), her grandmother's cousin Zlata Baker (centre) and her great-aunt Gitl Kantor. Romanov, Ukraine, circa early 1900s.

2   Malka's paternal uncle Baruch Bleinis and her aunt Manya Bleinis. Romanov, date unknown.

3   Malka's mother, Brindl (left), with a friend. Romanov, date unknown.

4   Malka's mother, Brindl, when she was a teenager. Romanov, date unknown.

1 Malka and her mother. Romanov, 1931.

2 Malka at approximately eight months old. Romanov, 1931.

3 Malka, age six. Romanov, 1937.

4 Malka, age seven. Romanov, 1938.

1

2

3

1 Malka and her mother, soon after the war. Romanov, circa 1946.

2 Malka (centre) with her baby brother Marik and Feiga Nogina, whom her family took in after the war. Romanov, circa 1947.

3 Malka (top left) visiting her paternal relatives who survived the war in Tashkent. In back, beside Malka, is her cousin Shlomo. Front (left to right): Malka's cousins Lev, Galina, Musia and a cousin, name unknown. Tashkent, Uzbekistan, circa 1946.

1 Malka with her friends from university. From left to right: Dina, Asya, Malka, Galina. Zhitomir, Ukraine, circa 1950.

2 Malka (front row, seated, far left) with her physical education class at Ivan Franko State University. Zhitomir, early 1950s.

1 & 2 Malka, age twenty-two. Zhitomir, 1953.

3 Malka and her husband, Efim (Efraim), at their wedding reception in his home-
town. Korosten, Ukraine, 1953.

1   Efim and Malka with their daughter Inna in the village where Efim was working
in the military. Bilokorovichi, Ukraine, 1961.
2   Malka and her daughters, Inna (left) and Galina (right). Bilokorovichi, circa 1962.
3   Inna (left) and Galina (right). Bilokorovichi, circa 1962.

1

2

1 Malka's brothers, Roman (left) and Marik (right), who were born after the war.
   Romanov, 1954.
2 Malka and Efim with their daughters, Galina and Inna. On the far left is Galina,
   the daughter of Nina Makarchuk, who helped Malka and her mother survive the
   Holocaust. Tashkent, 1965.

1

2

1 Nina Makarchuk, who gave refuge to Malka and her mother in Gvozdyarnya
(now Hvizdyarnya), Ukraine. Place and date unknown. Courtesy of Yad Vashem
Photo Archive, Jerusalem.

2 Lidia Kononchuk, who gave refuge to Malka and her mother in Monastyrok,
Ukraine. Place and date unknown. Courtesy of Yad Vashem Photo Archive, Jerusalem.

1

2

1 Malka and her family. Uzhgorod (now Uzhhorod), Ukraine, circa 1967.
2 Malka and her daughters, Inna (left) and Galina (right), before leaving Ukraine for Canada. Uzhgorod (now Uzhhorod), circa 1974.

1 Galina and her husband, Michael, at their wedding. Haifa, Israel, 1986.
2 Inna and her husband, Mark, celebrating their wedding. Calgary, March 23, 1995.

1

2

1   Malka with her daughters and her grandchildren. In back (left to right): Malka, Galina, Karin, Effie and Inna. In front, Solomon and Sophie. Vancouver, circa 2002.

2   Malka with her four grandchildren, celebrating Solomon's bar mitzvah. From left to right: Sophie, Effie, Malka, Solomon and Karin. Vancouver, 2012.

Malka Pischanitskaya. Vancouver, 2023.

Glossary

bris (Yiddish; covenant of circumcision) Judaism's religious ceremony to welcome male infants into the covenant between God and the Children of Israel through a ritual circumcision (removal of the foreskin of the penis) performed by a mohel, or circumciser, eight days after the baby is born. Traditionally, a baby boy is named after this ceremony.

Gestapo (German; abbreviation of Geheime Staatspolizei, the Secret State Police) The Nazi regime's brutal political police that operated without legal constraints to deal with its perceived enemies. The Gestapo was formed in 1933 and became a department within the SS in 1939. During the Holocaust, the Gestapo set up offices in Nazi-occupied countries and was responsible for rounding up Jews and sending them to concentration and death camps. They also arrested, tortured and deported those who resisted Nazi policies. A number of Gestapo members also belonged to the Einsatzgruppen, the mobile killing squads responsible for mass shooting operations of Jews in the Soviet Union.

Hannukah (Hebrew; dedication) An eight-day festival of lights, usually celebrated in December, that commemorates the victory of the Jews against the Syrian-Greek empire in the second century BCE. The festival is celebrated with the lighting of an eight-branched candelabrum called a menorah, or chanukiah, in remembrance of the rededication of the Temple in Jerusalem and the miracle of one day's worth of oil burning for eight days of light.

Hasidic (also Hasidism, Hasidim; from the Hebrew word hasid; pious person) A person or family belonging to an Orthodox Jewish spiritual movement founded by Rabbi Israel ben Eliezer (1698–1760), better known as the Baal Shem Tov, in eighteenth-century Poland. The Hasidic movement, characterized by philosophies of mysticism and focusing on joyful prayer, resulted in a new kind of leader who attracted disciples as opposed to the traditional rabbis who focused on the intellectual study of Jewish law.

kosher (Hebrew) Fit to eat according to Jewish dietary laws. Observant Jews follow a system of rules known as *kashruth* that regulates what can be eaten, how food is prepared and how animals are slaughtered. Food is kosher when it has been deemed fit for consumption according to this system of rules. There are several foods that are forbidden, most notably pork products and shellfish.

Levi Yitzchok of Berditchev An eighteenth century Hasidic master and teacher who lived in Poland and Ukraine. He was known for his love of the Jewish people and for seeing the sacredness in others and in everyday life. Rabbi Levi Yitzchok's book of reflections on the Torah, *Kedushat Levi* (Holiness of Levi), helped spread the Hasidic teachings.

matza (Hebrew) The crisp flatbread made of flour and water that is eaten during the holiday of Passover, when eating leavened foods is forbidden. Matza is eaten during the seder to commemorate the Israelites' slavery in Egypt and their redemption, when they left Egypt in haste and didn't have time to let their dough rise. *See also* Passover.

Orthodox The religious practice of Jews for whom the observance of Judaism is rooted in the traditional rabbinical interpretations of the biblical commandments. Orthodox Jewish practice is characterized by strict observance of Jewish law and tradition, such as the prohibition to work on the Sabbath and certain dietary restrictions.

Passover (in Hebrew, Pesach) An eight-day Jewish festival that takes place in the spring and commemorates the exodus of the Israelite slaves from Egypt. The festival begins with a lavish ritual meal called a seder, during which the story of the Exodus is told through the reading of a Jewish text called the Haggadah. During Passover, Jews refrain from eating any leavened foods. The name of the festival refers to God's "passing over" the houses of the Jews and sparing their lives during the last of the ten plagues, when the first-born sons of Egyptians were killed by God.

Purim (Hebrew; lots) The Jewish holiday that celebrates the Jews' escape from annihilation in Persia. The Purim story recounts how Haman, advisor to the King of Persia, planned to rid Persia of Jews, and how Queen Esther and her cousin Mordecai foiled Haman's plot by convincing the king to save the Jews. During the Purim festivities, people dress up in costumes, feast, read the story of Purim and send gifts of food and money to those in need.

Righteous Among the Nations A title given by Yad Vashem, the World Holocaust Remembrance Center in Jerusalem, to honour non-Jews who risked their lives to help save Jews during the Holocaust. A commission was established in 1963 to award the title. If a person fits certain criteria and the story is carefully checked, the honouree is awarded with a medal and certificate and is commemorated on the Wall of Honour at the Garden of the Righteous in Jerusalem.

Shabbos (Yiddish; Sabbath) The weekly day of rest beginning Friday at sunset and ending Saturday at nightfall, ushered in by the lighting of candles on Friday evening and the recitation of blessings over wine and challah (egg bread). A day of celebration as well as prayer, it is customary to eat three festive meals, attend synagogue services and refrain from doing any work or travelling.

shofar A ram's horn used as a trumpet during prayer services on the Jewish holiday of Rosh Hashanah and at the end of Yom Kippur. The four sounds made by the shofar symbolize a crying voice and evoke feelings of repentance, inspiring listeners to return to God.

shtetl (Yiddish) A mostly Jewish market town in Eastern Europe before World War II. Life in the shtetl revolved around Judaism and Jewish culture and was defined by the closely intertwined economic and social lives of its residents. Shtetls existed in Eastern Europe from the sixteenth century until they were wiped out in the Holocaust.

Star of David The six-pointed star that is the most recognizable symbol of Judaism. During World War II, Jews in Nazi-occupied areas were frequently forced to wear a badge or armband with the Star of David on it as an identifying mark of their lesser status and to single them out as targets for persecution.

Yad Vashem Israel's official Holocaust memorial centre and the world's largest collection of information on the Holocaust, established in 1953. Yad Vashem, the World Holocaust Remembrance Center, is dedicated to commemoration, research, documentation and education about the Holocaust. The Yad Vashem complex in Jerusalem includes museums, sculptures, exhibitions, research centres and the Garden of the Righteous Among the Nations.

Yiddish A language derived from Middle High German with elements of Hebrew, Aramaic, Romance and Slavic languages, and written in Hebrew characters. Spoken by Jews in east-central Europe for roughly a thousand years, it was the most common language among European Jews before the Holocaust. There are similarities between Yiddish and contemporary German.

Yitzchok, Levi. *See* Levi Yitzchok of Berditchev.

Index

adult survivors compared to children, xix–xx, 50
anti-Jewish laws, 23–25
antisemitism, xxi, 80, 90, 92
armbands, 23–24
art and memory, xxiii–xxiv, 101–102
Avraham (cousin), 30
Babii, Zina (friend), 45
Babushka. *See* Bleinis, Ruchel
Baker, Bronia (relative), 27–28, 30
Baker, Moshe (relative), 28
Baker, Zlata (relative), 27–28
Baras, Bronia, 75
Baras, Ita, 75
beliefs, importance of, xvii, xxi, xxv, 7, 11, 62, 65–66
Berdichev, 1, 4, 16
Berdychiv. *See* Berdichev
Bitman (doctor), 4
Bleinis, Brindl. *See* Brindl
Bleinis, Mendel (grandfather), 12
Bleinis, Ruchel, 12, 28
Blumental (Romanov shoemaker), 36
Bondarchuk (school director), 81–82

Bondarchuk, Galina, 89
Boruch (cousin), 30
Brindl (mother), 2; absence during early years, xvi; captured in Romanov, 37–40; escapes Romanov, 41–42; gives birth to sons, 86–87; in Gvozdyarnya, 71–79; in hiding in Romanov, 33–36; hunts collaborators, 84, 88; in Korchivka, 36–37; in Monastyrok, 62–70; moves to Israel, 92; offer of marriage from Josef Peck, 83; and trauma, 67; in Vienna, 93; in Yasnograd, 49–51
bris, 15–16
Canada, 93–104
Catholic Christians, 74–75
cattle sheds, as hiding places, 37, 47, 50–52, 56–57, 59–60, 70, 80
Chabad Lubavitch, 94
Chava. *See* Kantor, Hannah (Hill Kantor's wife)
Child Holocaust Survivor Group, xxiv, 101–102

The Azrieli Foundation was established in 1989 to realize and extend the philanthropic vision of David J. Azrieli, C.M., C.Q., M.Arch. The Foundation's mission is to support a wide spectrum of initiatives in education and research. The Azrieli Foundation is an active supporter of programs in the fields of education, the education of architects, scientific and medical research, and the arts. The Azrieli Foundation's many initiatives include: the Holocaust Survivor Memoirs Program, which collects, preserves, publishes and distributes the written memoirs of survivors in Canada; the Azrieli Institute for Educational Empowerment, an innovative program successfully working to keep at-risk youth in school; the Azrieli Fellows Program, which promotes academic excellence and leadership on the graduate level at Israeli universities; the Azrieli Music Project, which celebrates and fosters the creation of high-quality new Jewish orchestral music; and the Azrieli Neurodevelopmental Research Program, which supports advanced research on neurodevelopmental disorders, particularly Fragile X and Autism Spectrum Disorders.

The staff members dedicated to the Holocaust Survivor Memoirs Program are: Jody Spiegel, Arielle Berger, Catherine Person, Marc-Olivier Cloutier, Carson Phillips, Catherine Aubé, Matt Carrington, Devora Levin, Nadine Auclair, Michelle Sadowski, Elizabeth Banks, Monika Kolanka and Emily Standfield.